TARGET

Listening and Understanding in Secondary Schools

Meena Bahia-Tailor

TARGET

Listening and Understanding in Secondary Schools

Essential Reading for Effective Learning

For Class Teachers, SENCOs and
Support for Learning Staff

Meriel Davenport
and Philippa Hall

Barrington Stoke
Helen Arkell Dyslexia Centre

First published 2004 in Great Britain by Barrington Stoke Ltd,
Sandeman House, Trunk's Close, 55 High Street, Edinburgh, EH1 1SR

www.barringtonstoke.co.uk

ISBN 1-84299-157-4

Edited by Julia Rowlandson

Designed and typeset by GreenGate Publishing Services, Tonbridge
Printed in Hong Kong by Sino Publishing House Ltd

Contents

Introduction

Speech and language difficulties have many causes. While some children are diagnosed with specific disorders and have Individual Education Plans to address their needs, others remain undiagnosed and consequently fail to thrive either academically or socially.

Language is a complex process involving listening to and understanding speech, collating and storing information, and expressing ideas.

The aim of the book

In this book, we focus on the difficulties relating to the recognition and management of listening and understanding (language input) in the classroom and offer practical guidelines on how to help.

For simplicity, in this book the student is referred to as 'he' and the teacher as 'she'.

Terminology

Teachers may have encountered some of the following terminology relating to Speech and Language difficulties.

- **Receptive Language**: The understanding of spoken language, interpreting word meanings (*semantics*) and grammatical constructions (*syntax*).
- **Expressive Language**: The use of spoken language to convey ideas effectively.
- **Delayed Language**: A normally developing pattern of language but lagging behind levels expected of his age group.

- **Language Disorder (Dysphasia):** Where the normal processes of language development are altered.
- **Semantic–Pragmatic Disorder:** A difficulty in interpreting the meanings of words or sentences (*semantics*) and in using them appropriately in context (*pragmatics*).
- **Slow Processing:** An inability to interpret language at the speed at which it is presented.
- **Word retrieval (word finding) problems:** A difficulty accessing known vocabulary at will.
- **Auditory Short Term Memory:** The ability to hold auditory information long enough to interpret it. Some of this information will be stored in Long Term Memory, the rest will be lost.
- **Long Term Memory:** The storage of learned material.
- **Working Memory:** The ability to hold information in memory, while processing other related information, before completing the whole.
- **Figurative Language:** Language that cannot be interpreted literally, e.g. idioms, metaphors, similes, puns.
- **Non-verbal Language:** Body language, facial expression, gesture, tones of voice (often referred to as *intonation patterns*), volume; all of which are clues which contribute to communication.

Listening and understanding in the classroom

The processes involved in listening to and understanding spoken language are:

1. **Hearing:** The child must be able to hear adequately.
2. **Seeing:** The understanding of some features of non-verbal language relies on sight.
3. **Auditory perception:** The child needs to recognise speech sounds and know that they will convey meaning.

4 **Visual perception:** The child gains additional information by looking at the speaker and understanding non-verbal clues.

5 **Semantics:** The understanding of word meanings, including both concrete and non-concrete vocabulary.

example

Concrete – chair, running, hard.
Non-concrete – anxiety, feeling, delightful.

6 **Syntax:** The understanding of word order, including simple, compound and complex sentences.

example

Simple – The boy read the book.

Compound – The boy read the book before going to bed.
(2 sentences joined by a conjunction)

Complex – The boy, reading Harry Potter in the kitchen, was told by his mother to go to bed.
(clause inserted into main sentence)

7 **Figurative language:** The child needs to recognise that some language should not be interpreted literally.

example

Idiom – It's raining cats and dogs.
Simile – It came like a bolt from the blue.

Concept imagery and memory: The ability to use context and past experience in order to make sense of current information.

The child who has good concept imagery and memory is able to process information efficiently and make use of it in different contexts. He can build up connections between concepts, enabling him to collate, deduce, infer and recall.

The pupils this book can help

Some children with speech and language difficulties may have already been identified and are receiving professional help. Their problems may be only in the language area, or as an added dimension to another diagnosis, such as Dyslexia, Dyspraxia, Attention Deficit Disorder (ADD), Attention Deficit Hyperactivity Disorder (ADHD) and Autistic Spectrum Disorders (ASD) which includes Asperger Syndrome.

However, there are likely to be some children whose difficulties have not been diagnosed, and you may be the first person to recognise that their failure to thrive in the classroom is a result of poor listening and understanding.

If there is a child in your class about whom you are concerned, use **checklists 1 and 2** to pinpoint what you have observed and confirm your suspicions that there may be a listening and understanding problem.

Behaviours you may have noticed

- Poor eye contact.
- Long pauses before responding.
- Responds more readily to practical demonstration than to verbal instruction.
- Continual questioning for clarification, during television and video programmes.
- Quiet but passive member of the group. Despite an apparent willingness to please, performance is poor.
- Tendency to daydream. Particularly inattentive when listening to stories.
- Waits until another child responds and then copies, or waits to be offered help.
- Always says, 'I don't know/I can't do it'.
- Social isolation from other children.
- Diversionary tactics to mask difficulties; such as immature behaviour, asking needless questions, sharpening pencils, going to the toilet too frequently, etc.
- Distracts other children and/or is easily distracted.
- Negative attitude, including defiance, refusal, denial, confrontation, and/or belittlement of peers.
- Complains about other children's behaviour, while not recognising own unreasonable actions.
- Answers for others and interrupts.
- Frequent excuses for non-appearance of homework.
- Difficulty changing topic.
- Often perceives work as being within capabilities but then fails.
- Unwilling to accept correction about dogmatic opinions and/or lacks understanding of other people's points of view.
- Reported signs of stress from home, e.g. tantrums, unhappiness, etc.
- Fails to link cause and effect.

Poor responses to language of which you are aware

- Fails to respond, unless addressed by name.
- Poor understanding of vocabulary, both general and subject-specific.
- Responds inappropriately to questions.
- Forgets instructions.
- Inability to follow instructions accurately, particularly in less structured activities such as Games, Drama, Art, etc.
- Difficulty understanding compound or complex sentence constructions (see Chapter 3). Density of information may make this problem worse.
- Difficulty grasping underlying concepts, e.g. in Maths, though able to perform learned exercises.
- Specific difficulty in understanding written material.
- Inability to 'answer the question' in exams.
- Difficulty appreciating contextual clues.
- Literal understanding of figurative language, such as idioms, sarcasm, irony, metaphors and similes. Poor appreciation of jokes (see Chapter 8).
- Poor appreciation of time and calendar.
- Poor orientation in time and space, e.g. difficulty following timetable, reading maps.
- Difficulty understanding abstract concepts and words, e.g. fear, honour, delight.
- Difficulty identifying the main point. Inclined to focus on detail.

Management

Having identified those children with comprehension difficulties, the next step is to recognise how best to help them. While all teaching should be multi-sensory, an understanding of the child's preferred style of learning (*auditory*, *visual* or *kinaesthetic*) enables the teacher to make use of the child's strengths.

Auditory – through listening.
Visual – through seeing.
Kinaesthetic – through movement and practical activity.

Most children with difficulties in understanding, learn more effectively using kinaesthetic or visual means.

Language difficulties may cause gaps in earlier learning patterns, leading to basic misconceptions of which the teacher is unaware. It should not be assumed that underlying concepts are fully established and, where there are misunderstandings, it will be necessary to investigate where the breakdown has occurred and repair the damage. For example, David, aged 12, did not know the difference between a town, a county and a country and could not, therefore, begin to appreciate the concept of rural and urban population in the geography lesson.

The implications for the child

The implications of listening and understanding difficulties are varied and profound and can have significant effects on the success of the child's education because he:

- may miss much of a lesson, if a high proportion of the teaching is verbal

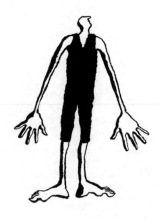

- may have difficulty understanding the rest of the lesson, if the introduction to a topic has not been grasped
- may be unable to retain any of the content, once the processing capacity is over-loaded
- may misunderstand what has been said and therefore be unable to make sense of what follows
- may not be aware of a topic change and so relate everything to the previous one
- may take another child's incorrect answer as fact
- may lose the thread of the content, if there is a distraction
- may be unable to transfer much verbal information to long term memory
- may not be able to listen as part of a group, needing to be addressed specifically by name
- may not be able to follow class discussions and conversation
- may not be able to transfer information from one environment to another
- may not be able to draw his own conclusions
- may have particular difficulty understanding subject-specific vocabulary
- may not be able to listen in an unstructured environment
- may have difficulty making and keeping friends
- may be physically aggressive, having mis-read the situation
- may have poor understanding of the language associated with number concepts
- may have poor understanding of money
- may have difficulty understanding written material
- may have difficulty with time management (see Chapter 6)
- may fail to identify the main point of an activity
- may be bogged down with detail

- may not learn unless activity is revised frequently
- may have difficulty taking concise notes
- may have a particular difficulty understanding poetic writing
- may have difficulty understanding another person's point of view
- may not read the signs which indicate that behaviour has 'gone too far'
- may have difficulty researching a topic
- may have difficulty judging what is relevant and irrelevant
- may have difficulty setting realistic goals.

How to use this book

In *Target Listening and Understanding* we start each chapter with a short introduction about the specific topic, then give some pointers for management, illustrative case studies, sample worksheets and suggested target cards. (The case studies have been taken from children in mainstream school, as well as pupils in a school for boys with specific learning difficulties.)

It should be noted that the worksheets are mostly for aural/oral use and not for written work.

Target cards are merely suggestions and can be adapted by the teacher to suit the needs of individual pupils. There is a target card template on page 10.

It is vital to remember that listening and understanding must be established, before literacy skills can be expected to develop and progress made at secondary level.

Remember to target small areas at a time with plenty of over-learning. It takes time to build up the strategies to enable the child to cope in the classroom.

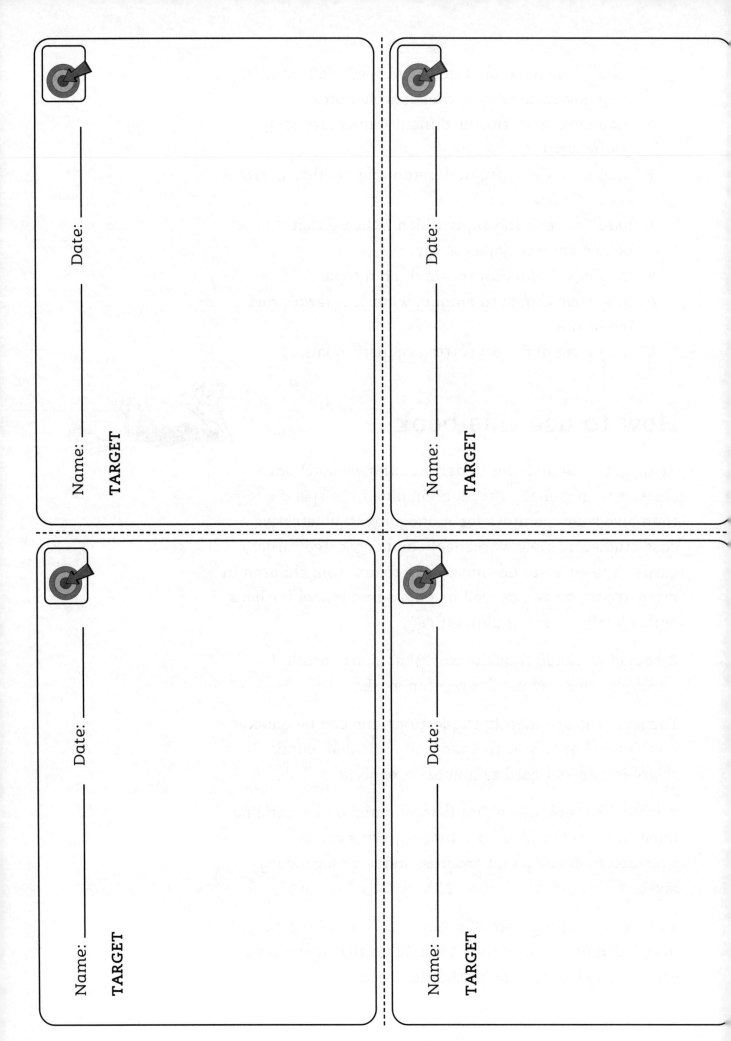

TARGET

Name: _____

Date: _____

TARGET

Name: _____

Date: _____

TARGET

Name: _____

Date: _____

TARGET

Name: _____

Date: _____

10

Listening Skills

A large part of education, particularly in secondary school, relies on the ability to listen to information presented orally. Listening skills break down when the child has difficulty processing the verbal material, because either it is presented too quickly or the language content is too complex.

The child who finds listening difficult may have learned to switch off. There is a danger of a downward spiral, since the less a child listens, the harder it becomes to understand the topic and the less incentive there is to make the effort to listen again. The child's belief in his ability begins to fade, as he fails to reach expected standards.

In order to break this cycle, he needs to re-learn that listening can be a rewarding experience. It must become an active process, for which he takes personal responsibility. An important part of this is developing the habit of watching the speaker, since some of the message is conveyed by facial expression and body language.

To help the child achieve listening success, it is important that the teacher backs up what is said with visual clues, such as pictures or demonstration, and that the tone of voice and the pacing of delivery are appropriate.

Some children find listening difficult because they are unable to filter out irrelevant background noise. They may not be able to disregard the whispered conversation at the back of the room in order to listen to the teacher's words. Such children are helped to focus by being reminded to look at the speaker.

Do:

- **Discuss the importance of listening.**
  Children cannot always judge whether or not they are listening, since they may not understand that it should be an active process.

- **Encourage the child to watch the speaker.**
  This ensures that the child is receiving the maximum information, both auditorily and visually.

- **Make sure the child is sitting near the teacher.**
  This makes it easier to look at the speaker.

- **Make sure the child is sitting where there are few distractions.**
  Allowing a child to sit near a window or at the back of the class may be unhelpful for good listening. Reduce distractions as much as possible.

- **Address the child by name to recall attention.**
  Some children need this personal prompt to help them focus on the speaker.

- **Give information in short, manageable chunks.**
  Too much information at once leads to a break down in listening skills.

- **Allow time for the child to process one piece of information before continuing.**
  Some children cannot listen to the next piece of information while processing the previous piece.

- **Give an overview of the lesson at the beginning.**
  This framework gives a structure to the lesson, which helps the child listen more actively. Tell the child roughly how long you are going to spend on each activity. The lesson will then not seem endless to him and will reinforce both the structure of the lesson and his understanding of time.

- **Summarise the content at the end of the lesson.**
  This reinforces the child's memory of what he has heard.

- **Give positive rewards for good listening.**
  For some children good listening should be seen as a goal in itself and given value. Rewards should be immediate and specifically related to the target.

example

- Well done, you looked at me while I was talking.
- Well done, you didn't turn round when Ben dropped his book.

- **Use alternative ways of attracting attention.**
  It is often more effective to use non-verbal ways to recall attention, such as quietly tapping the desk or touching the shoulder of a child who is no longer attending. A very effective strategy is to stop talking altogether, until the class as a whole is focused again on the teacher.

- **Make teaching child-centred whenever possible.**
  Children pay more attention when the subject relates to their own experience or interests.

- **Use multi-sensory techniques.**
  Wherever possible draw pictures to demonstrate your point, **while you are teaching**. If you are using prepared illustrations or diagrams, refer to them frequently. Practical demonstrations, acting and experiments all help to reinforce the listening aspect of the lesson.

- **Allow children to use activities which help them listen.**
  Some children find it easier to listen if they are allowed to do such things as doodling, drawing, using a 'fiddle toy', etc.

- **Ensure that children listen to contributions from other members of the class.**
  Some children fail to recognise that other pupils' contributions are an integral part of the lesson.

Case study 1

James, aged 11, was asked to listen to a short passage and answer questions. His initial reaction was to say that he was 'not good at this sort of thing.' Despite appearing to listen carefully and using good eye contact, he was only able to answer one question correctly. Another passage was read to him but this time he was given the questions first. He managed to answer four of the five questions.

Case study 2

Tom, aged 14, in a group with three other boys, was playing a game unfamiliar to all of them. The rules were explained and the game began. When it was his turn, he did not know what to do. He had failed to listen as a group member, needing his own personal explanation of the game.

Resources

1 Nanci Bell, *Visualizing and Verbalizing for Language Comprehension and Thinking*. Academy of Reading Publications (distributed by Taskmaster). ISBN 0-945-856-01-6

2 Graeme Beals, *Listening Comprehension – Middle and Upper*. Prim-Ed Publishing Pty. Ltd. ISBN Middle – 1-86400-039-2; Upper – 1-86400-040-6

3 Lynn Hutchison, *Reading Writing: Integrated Comprehension Skills*. Hodder and Stoughton. ISBN 0-340-54842-8

4 Jean Edwards, *Look, Listen and Think*. Prim-Ed Publishing Pty. Ltd. ISBN Lower – 1-86400-333-2; Middle – 1-86400-334-0; Upper 1-86400-335-9

5 Sandi Rickerby and Sue Lambert, *Listening Skills Key Stage 2*. Questions Publications Co. Ltd. ISBN 1-898149-461

Give the first two pieces of information and see if the child can suggest an appropriate answer. Then, give the third piece of information and see if he is able to change his mind if necessary.

If he experiences difficulty, break it down into smaller units.

- Fruit: it is yellow, it is round.

- Transport: it flies, it goes into space.

- Furniture: seats more than one, comfortable.

- Animal: lives in Africa, has a long neck.

- Vegetable: green, chopped up for eating.

- Electrical: used in the kitchen, heats up.

- Clothing: worn round the neck, keeps you warm.

- Footwear: worn in summer, made of leather.

- It shines, seen at night, in the sky.

- It shines, not hot, made of metal.

- Drink: it has milk in it, hot.

- Food: greasy, made of potato.

- It is worn, it has a face, for telling the time.

- Game: 11 in the team, you use a stick.

- Instrument: played with fingers, it is also a piece of furniture.

- It grows, may be decorated, it can be very tall.

- Insect: it flies, it lays eggs.

- To be looked through, you use 2 eyes, it makes things look bigger.

- To be read, printed every day, many pages.

- Made of wood, has 4 legs, may be polished.

Cont'd

- Electrical: it rings, you press it.

- Jewellery: it has a chain, worn round the wrist.

- Animal: may be eaten by people, has short legs.

- Vehicle: you pay a fare, it goes on rails.

- For reading, it tells you where to go, it has different colours.

- A home, made of wood, birds nest in it.

- Tool: for cutting, it has teeth.

- Made of plastic, holds rubbish, emptied once a week.

- Pet: has big ears, lives in a cage.

- Electrical: square, has coloured pictures.

- You eat it, it is oval, yellow and white inside.

- Transport: has wings, takes you on holiday.

- Clothing: tied in a knot, sometimes made of silk.

- Furniture: for sitting on, it has 3 legs.

- Very sweet, you eat it, bees make it.

- A city: the Queen lives there, the Thames flows through it.

- Liquid: has no taste, see-through.

- Liquid: keeps you alive, red.

- Country: in Europe, Britain fought 2 wars against it.

- Animal: quite small, has prickles.

- It burns, makes smoke, harmful to health.

- Clothing: has pockets, and 2 arms.

Read each sentence as many times as necessary, breaking it down into smaller chunks to help the child who processes slowly. The aim is always to give the child sufficient help to ensure he succeeds, while pushing the boundaries each time to improve his performance. Children do not learn simply through making mistakes!

● Aunt Mary grew some red flowers in her garden.

What did she grow?
What colour were the flowers?
Who grew them?

● What a dreadful day! The dog has been sick, John has broken the kitchen window and the car has a puncture.

Which window was broken?
What happened to the dog?
What other problem was mentioned?

● The two boys walked along by the railway track that ran through a dark little wood full of fir trees.

What did the boys walk beside?
What made the wood dark?
How many boys were there?

Cont'd

- The fat lady, carrying three large pink bags, sat down on the bus and spread herself over the seats on either side.

    How many bags were there?
    How many seats did she take up?
    Where was the fat lady?

- I thought I saw someone climbing into the upstairs bathroom window at number 45, so I called the police.

    What was the number of the house?
    At which window was the person climbing in?
    What did I do?

- The car screeched to a halt, narrowly missing the puppy which had run into the road after its master.

    Did the car stop?
    Who ran into the road?
    Why did the puppy run into the road?

- The day was crisp and frosty as Giles walked slowly over the fields with his spaniel.

    Who was with Giles?
    What was the weather like?
    What word was used to describe how Giles walked?

Listening Practice

Tell a story, slowly and carefully, stopping at crucial points to ask the child if he can think of a suitable word or phrase to continue the story. His idea may alter the direction of the story, but must be relevant to the information you have already given.

Take back the story quite quickly, and carry on, incorporating the child's ideas, until you come to another suitable point at which to stop.

Some possible story beginnings

When Jack opened the window, the rain blew in. The exercise books on his desk were soaked, and the ink had run, so that he was unable to read what he had written. Jack sighed. His teacher would be cross because...

The forest was silent. Not a leaf or a twig rustled. The boys kept very still, afraid that any movement would give them away. Suddenly they heard...

Kim was bored. Working in the music centre had sounded very exciting. She was interested in all sorts of music – jazz, rock, pop and even classical, but no one seemed to need her help or advice. The pay wasn't too good either. Just then a man stopped at the counter. He explained that he worked for a local radio show and was looking for someone young to help present the programme. 'What sort of programme?' Kim asked. 'Well,' said the man,...

Cont'd

The dog sat up and yawned. His owners were not yet awake, but he wanted to go out. The kitchen window was open, and he thought that if he jumped onto the table and then onto the sink, he could get out of the window. It was even easier than he had expected, but just as he reached onto the windowsill with his paws, ready to jump…

~•◆•~

Greg hit Tom. Tom hit him back, as hard as he could, and was pleased to see Greg fall back onto the sofa. 'Just wait!' bellowed Greg, and came running at him again. Tom had two seconds to decide what to do, then he…

~•◆•~

Harry watched the plane circling lazily in the air. He could hear the gentle, continuous sound of its engine above the noise of the boys playing round him. Then the noise stopped. Looking up he saw…

~•◆•~

Jim and Lucy looked at the shopping list. There seemed to be an awful lot of things on it. Outside the shop, the day was sunny and hot, and they could see some friends passing by on their way to the swimming pool. They looked at each other, both thinking that they could always do the shopping later…

Listening Games

I went to market

A game most people already know.

The teacher starts with 'I went to market and bought a ...' (choose an item, e.g. an apple).

The child next in the circle says 'I went to market and bought an apple and ...' (adds another item, e.g. a walking stick). This carries on round the group until the list to be remembered is too long, and everyone gives up.

The children must look and listen to each other, to give themselves as many clues as possible, and should be encouraged to try to visualise all the items as a back-up to auditory memory. Use gesture, or give sound cues, to help the children to succeed. Set a target of how many items you think they might remember. Let them give each other clues to keep the game going.

The same game can be varied by only having items which belong to the same category, or using alphabetical order.

Listening for category words

Tell the child you are going to list some words and you want him to stop you each time you give a particular category word.

For example, in the following set of words you may ask him to listen for:

- **Colours:** bat, banana, snake, *orange*, cup, drawing pin, *purple*, *red*, balloon, table.
- **Size:** hot, far, think, *long*, wish, single, *metre*, *large*, cool, fat.
- **Food:** *cream*, fan, button, monkey, *lettuce*, fork, *crab*, *orange*, *fish*.

Cont'd

Simon says

This is another old favourite, where the teacher gives the children an instruction (such as 'hands on heads', 'stand on one leg') preceded by 'Simon says'. If the teacher does not say 'Simon says', then the child must not obey.

A harder variation (both for the teacher and for the child!) is for the teacher to give a verbal instruction, while demonstrating a different action. The child must *listen* and not copy.

Who's right?

This is a group game. The children stand in the centre, with one side of the room for 'yes' answers, and the other side for 'no' answers. The teacher prepares a list of questions which she asks the children. They must decide whether the answer is 'yes' or 'no' and go to the appropriate side of the room. The children with wrong answers are eliminated from the game.

Who said what?

This is suitable for a small group of children. The teacher asks each child where he has been on holiday, or his favourite colour, sport or food, or some family details. The children are then questioned about what each other has said.

The Spoon Game

A game for listening.

This game is simply intended to make listening fun. Any short story may be used with any choice of target word. In the original game, spoons are used, but corks or soft balls make a possibly safer alternative.

The children sit in a circle, with their hands on their heads. In the centre of the table are a number of spoons, one less than the number of children, on the same principle as musical chairs.

The story is read. Each time the word SPOON is said, the children have to grab a spoon. If a child takes a spoon, without the word being used, he is out. The winner is the child with the last spoon.

The story should contain 'traps' where the target word is expected, but not used, or where words with similar sounds are used.

Example of a story

Once upon a time there were three goblins who lived in a hole under a tree. The hole was dark and dank and very smelly because the goblins never cleaned it. They never washed up either, leaving dirty cups, plates, knives, forks and **SPOONS** all over the place. Actually there weren't many knives, forks and eating implements around because these horrible goblins didn't use any. They just crammed everything into their mouths with their very dirty hands; except for soup, of course. You have to eat soup with special tools, otherwise it all drops down your front, making your shirt damp and disgusting, so **SPOONS** were sometimes useful.

Cont'd

One of the goblins' mothers gave them a large box of crockery – and **SPOONS** – but they used the plates to throw at each other, the cups as footballs and the **SPOONS** as cricket bats. These spare items were quickly chipped or bent so that they were no use for eating off or with.

Another of the goblins' mothers gave them pots and pots of jam, which they scooped out with a knife. Sometimes they cut their tongues doing this, which just shows how silly it is to eat with a knife rather than something else – like a **SPOON**.

The third goblin's mother was too mean to give them anything, in fact she used to sneak round and steal things from them – especially **SPOONS** – which she sold at the Goblin **SPOON** Market, for a spectacularly high price.

These three goblins were always quarrelling and being spiteful to each other. Every so often they fought so much that they had to make the hole bigger, so that they could keep away from each other. And what did they use to dig out earth? Spades, of course, and **SPOONS**. The hole under the tree became bigger and bigger. One day they were digging yet more holes and hitting each other over the head with **SPOONS** and spades, kicking each other, pulling hair and stamping on feet, when there was a huge crash and the tree fell down, squashing all the goblins and their belongings – particularly the **SPOONS**. So that was the end of them.

Name: _____ Date: _____

TARGET

Are you listening?

Ask for repetitions.

Asking ☐☐☐☐☐☐☐☐☐

Name: _____ Date: _____

TARGET

What helps me to listen?

Looking at the teacher ☐
Taking notes ☐
Doodling ☐
Fiddle toy ☐

Name: _____ Date: _____

TARGET

Watch and listen to the teacher.

Name: _____ Date: _____

TARGET

No interruptions.

Period 1 ○○○○○○○○
Period 2 ○○○○○○○○
Period 3 ○○○○○○○○

Following Instructions

A child's failure to follow instructions may be the first indication to a teacher that the pupil has listening and processing difficulties. This may be for a number of reasons, including the length of the instruction, the *density of information*, the complexity of vocabulary or *syntax*, or the order of the wording.

> **Density of information** – the amount of essential information in a phrase or sentence.
> **Syntax** – the order of words in a sentence.

Length of instruction

Consideration should be given to the length of the instruction. The child may be confused by too much information, some of which may have little direct relevance to the actual instruction. The child may only have the capacity to take in the first or last part of the instruction, or may focus only on individual words or phrases, regardless of their relative importance.

Density of information

The density of information given in a sentence should also be taken into account. If a single sentence has a high proportion of important words, the child may not have sufficient time to process each part. The danger is that the child picks up two unrelated parts of the instruction and joins them to create a new, incorrect concept.

Another possibility is that the overload of information may erase the entire instruction.

Vocabulary

It is important that vocabulary used in instructions is familiar to the child. There can be unexpected gaps in core vocabulary. For example, sequential words such as *before* and *after*, and prepositions such as *in front of* and *between*, may not be fully understood, even at secondary level (see Chapter 5 – Vocabulary).

Syntax

Consideration should be given to the syntactic (grammatical) structure. Many children do not understand complex sentences, involving *embedded phrases* or *clauses*.

Embedded phrase or **clause** – an additional phrase or clause, which occurs in the middle of a sentence, e.g. John, who was carrying a bag, caught the bus.

They may also have difficulty understanding some grammatical structures, such as the *passive* voice or *sequential concepts* (see Chapter 3 – Syntax).

Active – The man hit the dog.
Passive – The dog was hit by the man.

Since most information contained in instructions is both concrete and logical, it is possible to help these children to be more successful, by giving them strategies to compensate, such as making a mental picture, repeating the instruction to themselves, or asking for clarification.

Do:

- **Give information in short manageable chunks.**
  Overloading the child's memory with too much information at once may mean that he loses the whole instruction or becomes confused. This may lead to the downward spiral of listening seeming pointless (see Chapter 1).

- **Draw and/or demonstrate where possible.**
  Backing up aural information with a visual stimulus will help the child not only to understand but also to retain what you are telling him.

- **Sequence logically.**
  Many children become confused when the instruction is not given in the same order as its expected response. For example, in the instruction 'before you go outside to break, hand in your work to Mr Jones next door', the child may go outside first, thinking that he should hand in his work after break.

- **Be prepared to repeat or rephrase your instruction.**
  When an instruction has not been fully understood, it will be necessary to either repeat the same wording or rephrase the instruction in a simpler way. Generally speaking, repetition helps the child who processes accurately but slowly, while rephrasing is useful for those who have weak understanding of vocabulary or syntax.

- **Use short sentences.**
  Longer sentences which include non-essential information may only serve to confuse the listener. Identifying the relative importance of words and ideas is often challenging for these children, as in 'Don't forget to bring your kit for the match and you must remember to collect your packed lunch and of course I would like your homework handed in as usual.'

- **Limit the amount of information in your instruction.**
  Too much information included in a single instruction may overload the child's processing abilities. For example, 'Bring the large test tubes from Lab 2 that are between the clamps and the goggles', requires the child to process five separate pieces of information, which are each of equal importance.

- **Help the child to find a compensatory strategy.**
  (a) Visualisation
  Ask the child to picture himself carrying out the instruction as you give it, thus making use of visual memory, as a back-up to the auditory pathway. This skill has to be practised, until the child automatically backs up the verbal input with visualisation.

  (b) Sub-vocalisation
  The child may be helped to process the instruction, by repeating it quietly to himself.

  (c) Asking for clarification
  Knowing when and how to ask for clarification is a sign of active listening and should be encouraged (see Chapter 1).

Case study 1

Ellen, aged 13, was asked in the morning to deliver an envelope to the school office. The teacher then said, 'Clear up the paints before you go.' The second instruction completely erased the memory of what she was to do with the envelope and by the end of the day she was still holding it.

Case study 2

Jonathan, aged 14, was told in ICT to save his work in a particular format on the main server. Despite understanding how to undertake each individual computing process, he was totally unable to respond because of the density and speed of presentation. As he had taken in no information at all, he could not even ask for clarification and was afraid to admit it.

Resources

1   Nanci Bell, *Visualizing and Verbalizing for Language Comprehension and Thinking*. Academy of Reading Publications (distributed by Taskmaster). ISBN 0-945-856-01-6

2   Jean Edwards, *Look, Listen and Think*. Prim-Ed Publishing Pty. Ltd. ISBN Lower – 1-86400-333-2; Middle – 1-86400-334-0; Upper – 1-86400-335-9

3   Sandi Rickerby and Sue Lambert, *Listening Skills Key Stage 2*. Questions Publications Co. Ltd. ISBN 1-898149-461

4   Graeme Beals, *Listening Comprehension – Middle and Upper*. Prim-Ed Publishing Pty. Ltd. ISBN Middle – 1-86400-039-2; Upper – 1-86400-040-6

5   Sally Merrison and Andrew John Merrison, *Merrimaps*. STASS Publications. ISBN 1-874534-35-7

6   Joanne Carlisle, *Reasoning and Reading*. Educators Publishing Service Inc. ISBN Level 1 – 0-8388-1813-7; Level 2 – 0-8388-1814-5

Double Instructions

Each of these instructions has at least two parts to listen to.

1 Put your name at the top of the page in the middle.

2 Put the date in the left-hand corner at the top of the page.

3 Number your page at the bottom on the right-hand side.

4 Look at the opening sentence of the third paragraph on page 43.

5 Draw a circle beside the triangle and under the square.

6 Write your name half-way down the page, 5 cm in from the margin.

7 Draw a fence in front of a tree and behind a house.

8 Write down three 2-syllable words which begin with 't'.

9 Draw a picture of a person looking to his left.

10 Write the letter x to the right of a vertical line.

Now you must also listen for the things you must not do.

1 Draw a circle and a cross that is not below it.

2 Write your first name and surname but not your middle name.

3 Draw three circles with triangles inside but not the usual way up.

4 Write your name on the page but not at the top.

5 Write down your telephone number but not the area code.

6 Write down three words that begin with 'b' but do not end in 't'.

7 Draw a picture of a house but without a chimney or TV aerial.

8 Write the names of all your family but not your own name.

9 Write the months of the year but not those beginning with 'j'.

10 Write the days of the week but not in the right order.

Number Grid

24	49	12	19	123	40	22	3	39	65
17	21	342	200	75	51	15	25	47	72
5	29	56	18	31	85	232	74	90	104
28	46	79	84	63	41	37	94	55	16
325	6	99	183	42	35	11	4	34	2
49	62	106	33	284	10	1	92	71	66
29	45	91	74	42	36	39	28	72	240

Instructions

Level A: *Which number is:* above, below, before, after, next to, in front of, behind, to the left of, to the right of ...?

Level B: *Which number is:* horizontal to, vertical to, diagonal to, between, 3 in front of, 2 behind, 4 above ...?

Level C: *Which number is:* between 6 and 42 and above 33; diagonal to 18 and below 40; in the third line and vertically above 33 ...?

Level D: *Which number is:* in the line below 5, above 10 and diagonal to 11; before 4, to the right of 6 and vertically above 74 ...?

Level E: Start at 5, go 3 squares to the right, vertically up 2 squares, and diagonally down 1 square to the left. What number is it?

Level F: *What is the answer?* Add 3 to the number which is between 35 and 34 and vertically below 25; twice the number to the right of 24 which is in the third column.

Making use of visualisation to help listening

Ask the child to pretend he is going to follow treasure hunt clues.

He must picture in his mind the directions you are going to give him.

At the end you will ask him to tell back to you all the instructions, or you might ask him questions about one piece only.

Example

You are standing in front of a red door. **Picture the red door in your mind**. Open the door, step through it and turn left. **Picture yourself turning left**. You are on a gravel path which runs between two tall hedges. **Picture it**. At the end of the path there is a gate which leads into a wood. **Picture it**. All the trees have grey trunks. Half-way through the wood you come to a small lake. **Picture it**. On the lake are three small rowing boats. One is yellow, one is orange and green, and one is brown. **Picture the boats**. Untie the orange and green boat, and row to the other side of the lake. **What colour boat are you in? Picture it**. Leave the boat and continue walking through the wood, till you come to a tree right on the far side of the wood. You must climb the tree, but be very careful because some of the branches are rotten. **Picture it**. Climb up to the third branch. **Picture it**. At the base of the branch is a hole in the trunk. Put your hand inside, and you will find a heavy metal key, wrapped in purple velvet. **Picture it**. Climb back down the tree, but do not put your weight on the first branch because it might give way.

Cont'd

Next, you must climb the hill which you can see in front of you, because from the top of the hill you can see the castle. **Picture it**. When you reach the castle, give the gatekeeper the password 'Trellisort'. **Think what the password sounds like**, write it in your mind. The gatekeeper will open the gate and let you in. Take the left-hand staircase, go though the pink door into a large room with a cupboard in the far right-hand corner. **Picture it**. Open the cupboard, look on the second shelf, in the extreme right-hand corner – and there you will find the treasure!

Initially, the child will need constant reminders to picture the story. With practice, he will start to do so automatically. Give enough reminders to ensure that he cannot fail.

Either ask him to re-tell the instructions, or ask specific questions:

- What colour was the door?

- What was at the end of the path?

- How many boats were there?

- Why must you be careful climbing the tree?

- What was the key wrapped in?

- How could you see the castle?

- What was the password?

- What is the last sound in the password?

- How many doors did you have to go through to get to the treasure?

- In which corner of the shelf was the treasure?

- What might the treasure have been?

Barrier Activities

Teachers' instructions

Drawing to instruction

(See Sheet 2.4a)

Make a series of cards with numbers, letters or simple line drawings on them. The child sits where he cannot see the card and attempts to follow the verbal instructions you give him. The two drawings are then compared.

Ten differences

(See Sheet 2.4b)

Both you and the child have a copy of the same picture, and sit so that the child cannot see your version. Make ten changes to your picture and instruct the child to make these changes on his copy.

In both of these exercises, the child may ask for clarification, but this should be given verbally without gesture or pointing. If the child still cannot follow the instruction, the activity should be stopped and an explanation, with demonstration and practice, given on another, similar example. The aim is that when the exercise is resumed, the child will then be able to carry out the instruction.

Cont'd

Drawing to instruction

1 Draw a cross in the top left-hand corner.
2 Draw a circle in the top right-hand corner.
3 Half-way down the right-hand side, draw a square.
4 Draw a triangle half-way along the bottom edge of your paper.

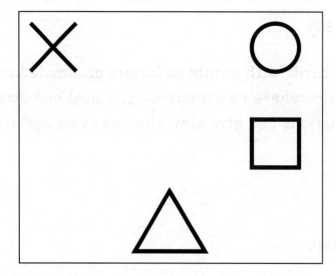

1 Draw a circle in the middle of the page.
2 Draw an equals sign in the middle at the top.
3 Between the circle and the equals sign draw a square.
4 To the left of the circle draw a triangle.
5 Below the triangle draw another circle.

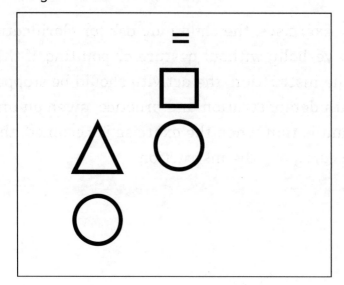

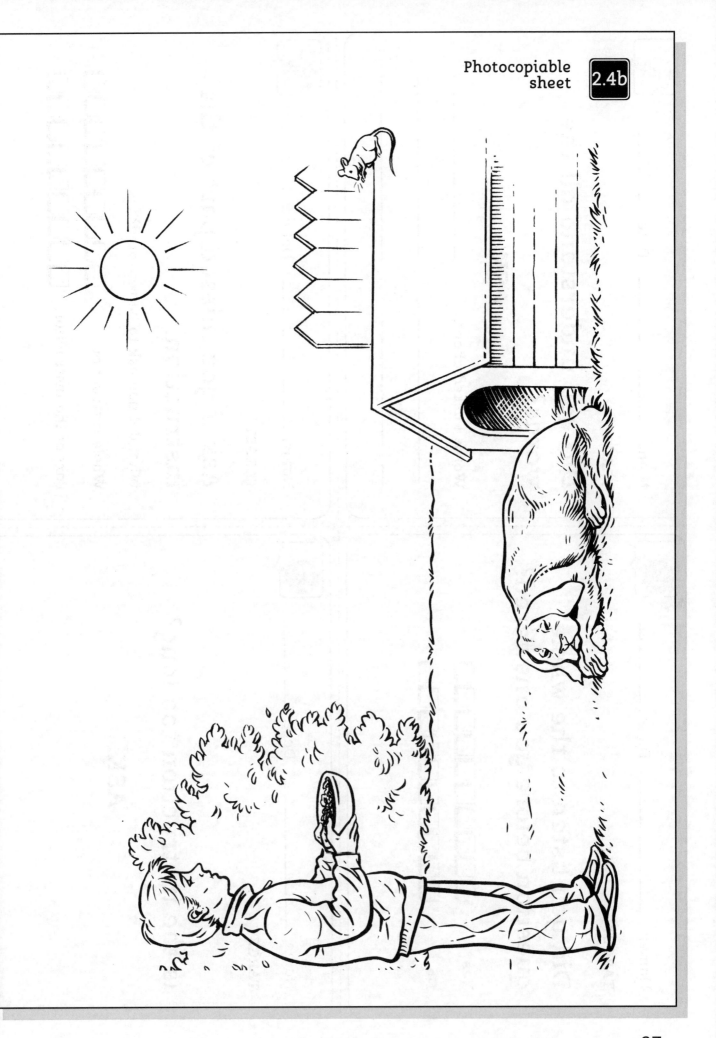

TARGET

Did you understand all the words?

ASK!

Words I asked about:

_____

_____

_____

Name: _____

Date: _____

TARGET

Ask if you missed part of the instruction.

What did you ask to be repeated?

Whole instruction ☐☐☐☐☐☐☐

Part of the instruction ☐☐☐☐☐☐☐

Name: _____

Date: _____

TARGET

Did you listen to the whole question before you answered?

Yes ☐☐☐☐☐☐☐☐

No ☐☐☐☐☐☐☐☐

Name: _____

Date: _____

TARGET

Is the instruction too long?

ASK!

Name: _____

Date: _____

Syntax

Some children, whose understanding of vocabulary is good, may be confused by the structure of the sentence.

Simple sentence constructions do not normally cause a problem. *Compound sentences*, however, may be more difficult to process. Conditional clauses, involving words such as **if**, **although** and **unless**, can also be confusing.

> **Compound sentences** – two simple sentences joined by a conjunction.

Comprehension often breaks down when *complex sentences* are used, involving embedded clauses and phrases.

For example, when the child with language processing difficulties, hears the instruction 'Put the bike, which is green, on the car', he may assume that it is the car which is green rather than the bike.

> **A complex sentence** – one which includes a main clause and one or more subordinate clauses.

The child may be unable to identify the main topic of the sentence, where subordinate clauses are used. It may not be clear, in the sentence 'Mr Jones, who is the bank manager, fell in the river', whether the important point is that he is good with money or that he got wet!

Word order is crucial to the meaning of a sentence. The subject and object in a simple sentence can only be correctly interpreted by their position, relative to the verb. For example, 'The car hit the train' has a different meaning to 'The train hit the car'. Similarly, the difference between a statement and a question may only be the word order. 'The boy is late' and 'Is the boy late?' require different responses from the listener.

Negative constructions often pose problems in understanding. It is much easier to interpret 'Find something large and light' than 'Find something large but not heavy'.

Similarly, *neither ... nor* is more difficult to understand than *either ... or*.

The passive voice is often confusing because the child, who does not process syntax easily and is unfamiliar with the more complex verb construction, disregards the word '*by*'. The child may be unable to decide who was 'seeing' in 'Mary was seen by Tom'.

> **Active** – Tom saw Mary.
> **Passive** – Mary was seen by Tom.

Do:

- **Be aware of the need to use simple or compound sentences.**
  If a child is having difficulty understanding a general concept, the language and the syntax (structure of the sentence) used in the explanation should be as simple as possible.

- **Practise the use of subordinating conjunctions.**
  The child may misunderstand the implications of conjunctions such as: *if, although, until, unless, whenever, before, while, because*.

- **Practise finding the main topic of the sentence.**
  By identifying the main topic of the initial sentence, the child is more likely to understand subsequent information.

- **Practise finding the main topic of the paragraph.**
  When the syntax is misunderstood in a single sentence, the child may become confused about the overall content.

- **Give instructions involving more than one clause in a logical order.**
  See Chapter 2 – Following Instructions.

- **Use positive constructions.**
  Using negatives adds an extra burden for the child with processing difficulties.

- **Use active constructions.**
  The passive tense involves both a change in word order and an increase in the number of words to be processed.

Case study 1

Alice, aged 11, when told 'Write letters of the alphabet around the square but not on the top surface', repeatedly tried to write the letters on the top surface. Each time she was stopped, and the instruction was repeated, with the emphasis on the word not. Finally, she said in frustration, 'I keep trying to do what you told me and you won't let me.'

Case study 2

Matthew, aged 13, when hearing the sentence, '"Here is your breakfast," said Karen, "and remember to take your medicine"', thought that Karen was the person being given breakfast. Despite being told that he had misunderstood, he was unable to change his interpretation, until the third attempt.

Resources

1 Joanne Carlisle, *Reasoning and Reading*. Educators Publishing Service Inc. ISBN Level 1 – 0-8388-1813-7; Level 2 – 0-8388-1814-5

2 Marilyn M Toomey, *Expanding and Combining Sentences*. Winslow. ISBN 0-923573-28-3

Matching Clauses

Can you decide which clause matches the beginning of the sentence?

The dog barked loudly	we still did not have enough to buy the digital camera.
The boy broke his leg	Mr Smith will not mark it.
Even though we had saved up for three months	as a result of the unusually wet weather.
John got up early that day	before going home to cook supper.
As we came nearer to the house	because he had heard the front door opening.
If we don't hand in our work by the weekend	we will not be ready to perform the play.
Many of our matches were cancelled	when he fell over, while learning to ski.
I went to the supermarket	so he was sure that he would get to school on time.
Unless we rehearse every day	I still cannot bear Brussels sprouts.
Although I like most vegetables	we could just see a light shining through the fog.

Getting the Main Idea

Which is the main idea in each sentence?

1 Riding her bike home, Lucy saw four boys skateboarding in the park.

2 Sam was crossing the main road, when the fire engine raced past.

3 I cannot go to see the film, until I finish my homework.

4 If the dog runs for that ball, he will trample down the flowers.

5 Even though we wanted to eat a pizza, we only had enough money for a plate of chips.

6 Unless you hand in your work on time, it will not be marked before the weekend.

7 He continued to work hard, even after the bell for break had rung.

8 The girls did not enjoy the programme because it was too old-fashioned.

9 Before I tell you the secret, you must promise not to tell anyone else.

10 Waiting for her friend at the shop, Anna thought about the things she wanted to buy.

11 Whenever the bell goes, Sam is always the first to leave the room.

12 I was really hungry, so I bought a Chinese meal.

13 Despite the dreadful weather, they decided to set out on their journey.

14 They decided to go to see the film, before they went to the party.

15 Having visited the museum, they decided to go home before dark.

16 We had to drive quite quickly because we did not want to lose sight of the van in front.

17 The policeman warned the boys, even though they were very young.

18 When we were going on holiday, we had to go to the station first, in order to catch the train to the airport.

19 The boy was wearing a sling because he had broken his arm, while playing in a rugby match.

20 I will go along with whatever you all decide.

1 George jumped last in the competition.

   George jumped in the last competition.

2 It seems that whenever we go to school, it is raining.

   It always seems to rain when we go to school.

3 Some of the children spent all their money at the fair.

   All the children spent some of their money at the fair.

4 Mr Jones stood next to his mother and father.

   Mr Jones stood between his mother and father.

5 John has as many sweets as Max.

   John and Max have the same amount of sweets.

6 Neither of the girls wanted to see the film.

   Both the girls preferred not to see the film.

7 Most dogs are kind and gentle and make good pets.

   Dogs make good pets because they are kind and gentle.

8 Mr Evans always washes his car on Sunday.

   Mr Evans only washes his car on Sunday.

Cont'd

9 Even though they knew it was dangerous, they ran across the busy road.

They ran across the busy road, despite knowing the dangers.

10 We live in the fifth house, after the garage on the left.

We live in the house that is fifth on the left, after the garage.

11 Sarah could not afford to go to the theme park with her friends.

The theme park was too expensive for Sarah to go with her friends.

12 After they had been bowling, they ate a pizza.

They went bowling, then they ate a pizza.

13 Before they went bowling, they ate a pizza.

They ate a pizza, then they went bowling.

14 It was such a lovely day, so we decided to go to the beach.

Because it was such a lovely day, we decided to go to the beach.

15 Mr Black enjoys making all kinds of furniture in his workshop.

Mr Black enjoys making chairs and tables in his furniture workshop.

16 Jodie is the only girl in the class to go abroad on holiday.

Jodie only goes abroad on holiday.

1   The man, who wore a grey coat, stroked the cat.
    Whose coat was grey?

2   Bill's energetic dog ran across Mr White's field.
    Who owned the dog?
    Who owned the field?

3   My sixty-year-old mother had a brother, who lived in Australia.
    Who was sixty years old?
    Who lived abroad?

4   When Tom arrived at the office, he was phoned by a man with a
    deep voice.
    Who went to the office?
    Who had a deep voice?
    Who made the phone call?

5   The woman, whose trolley was full, stood behind me in the queue.
    Who had a full trolley?
    Who was first in the queue?

6   Mrs Jones from West Street, who has a daughter living in Lower
    Road, works in the library.
    Who lives in West Street?
    Who lives in Lower Road?
    Who is the mother?
    Who works in the library?

7   The four boys, in the red and white strip, beat the boys in blue in
    the relay.
    Who failed to win the race?
    How many were in each team?

8   The girl with the long blond hair was sitting behind the dark girl,
    who was wearing glasses.
    Who wore glasses?
    Who was sitting in front?
    Who had long hair?

Name: —————————— Date: ——————————

TARGET

What is the main point of the paragraph?

Name: —————————— Date: ——————————

TARGET

How many ideas are there?

Name: —————————— Date: ——————————

TARGET

Did I understand everything?

Yes ☐☐☐☐☐☐☐☐☐☐

No ☐☐☐☐☐☐☐☐☐☐

Not sure ☐☐☐☐☐☐☐☐☐☐

Name: —————————— Date: ——————————

TARGET

What is the main point of the sentence?

Do you know? If not, ASK!

© M Davenport & P Hall 2004   Listening and Understanding in Secondary Schools   3 Syntax

Understanding Question Words

4

Although children answer questions from a young age, their understanding must develop, as the complexity of the questions increases and more specific answers are required. The child needs to understand the expectations of the different question words. For instance, when asked '*who?*' the answer must include a person; '*why?*' elicits a reason and '*when?*' a time.

It cannot be assumed that children with language processing difficulties understand what each question word is asking. Despite understanding the content, they may still answer the question incorrectly.

'Why' is probably the most difficult question word because the answer involves reasoning. The child should be helped to understand that there may be more than one answer, none of which is incorrect.

In exams, children often fail to answer the question specifically. This is therefore a crucial skill and should be taught initially through oral language.

Do:

- **Undertake specific work on question words.**
  The child needs to learn what sort of answer is expected from each question word.

- **Require an accurate response.**
  The child should answer the question you have asked without giving more information than is required.

- **Encourage the child to consider alternative answers to 'why' questions.**
  This is often the start of reasoning and helps the child to see that there may be different, but equally reasonable, point of view.

Case study 1

Craig, aged 12, when asked 'Why did the girl shout for help?' replied 'Because the boy has fallen in the water.' When asked again 'So why did she shout for help?', he repeated rather indignantly 'Because the boy has fallen in the water.' He was unable to develop his answer further.

Case study 2

Georgina, aged 13, when asked what a Bunsen burner is used for, answered 'It burns gas through a tube.'

Resources

Luanne Martin, *Think It – Say It*. Communication Skill Builders. ISBN 0-88450-570-7

Match the answers to the questions

Answers

- None today, thank you.

- In case it rains.

- 10 o'clock.

- Four for me and two for my brother.

- We're going to the cinema.

- I tripped over the dog.

- Auntie, and maybe grandma, if she's well enough.

- There was a traffic jam on the road to school.

- I think she's ill.

- I'd like to go swimming.

Questions

- Who is coming for lunch?

- How did you break that cup?

- What time is it?

- How many pints of milk do you want?

- Why did you bring your coat?

- What do you want to do?

- How many do you want?

- Where are you going this afternoon?

- What's the matter with Jane?

- What made you late for school?

Another way of asking questions

Turn these statements into questions.

- The dog is black.

- The boys are playing in the stream.

- John did go to school yesterday.

- You could buy some plums instead of some apples.

- We can go swimming on the way home.

- This is how you tie a reef knot.

- You will tidy the room.

Cont'd

Think of some questions to go with these answers

- 11.

- 33, Chestnut Road, Reading, Berkshire.

- My brother.

- It might be in the fridge.

- Between 3 p.m. and 5 p.m.

- My friend went there last year and told us about it.

- In the cupboard.

- Turn the handle to the right.

- Because I need to earn some money.

- You haven't turned the switch on.

- In September.

- Reading a book.

- The old lady at number 7.

- I don't know.

- Look in the yellow pages.

- I can't remember.

- It's collapsed in the middle.

- When you're 17.

- Because it's raining.

- Because I'm older than you.

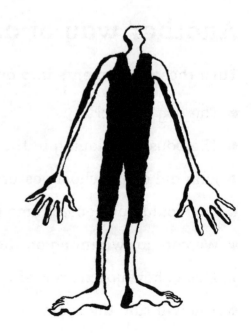

Question Words

Look at the picture on the following sheet (Sheet 4.2a) and answer the questions. This activity can be repeated at a variety of levels and using more complex pictures.

1   **Who** is holding the young child's hand?
    Why is she holding the child's hand?
    How is the child feeling?
    Where are they going?
    What has happened to the child?

2   **Who** is looking at his watch?
    Why is he looking at his watch?
    Where is he sitting?
    What is he waiting to do?

3   **Who** is eating a sandwich?
    Why is he eating a sandwich?
    Where did he buy it?
    What sort of sandwich is he eating?
    When do you eat a sandwich?
    How is he sitting?

4   **Who** is having a picnic?
    Where are they having their picnic?
    What are they having for their picnic?
    What are they sitting on?
    Why are they having a picnic?
    When will they go home?
    How will they go home?

5   **Who** wants to chase the ducks?
    Why does he want to chase the ducks?
    What will happen if he chases the ducks?
    How can his owner stop him chasing the ducks?
    Where are the ducks going?

Name: _____ **Date:** _____

TARGET

Is the reason you have given possible?

Have you checked? □□□□□□□□□

Name: _____ **Date:** _____

TARGET

What sort of question is this?

Who? □	Where? □
What? □	When? □
Why? □	How? □

Name: _____ **Date:** _____

TARGET

Have you answered the question you were asked?

Have you checked? □□□□□□□□□

Name: _____ **Date:** _____

TARGET

Is everything you have said relevant to the question?

Have you checked? □□□□□□□□□

Vocabulary

5

Many children with specific learning difficulties have very poor understanding of vocabulary. There are a number of reasons for this, but the main ones are:

- Intermittent hearing loss in the early years prevents the young child from developing his vocabulary.
- Children who process slowly are deprived of the reinforcement necessary to establish word meaning.
- Children who rarely read also miss the reinforcement of vocabulary.

The understanding of vocabulary is built up by hearing the word used in a variety of contexts and situations. If the child fails to understand the early vocabulary and concepts, he is unable to underpin his understanding of later word meanings. The development of vocabulary follows a hierarchical structure, and unless the lower order words are firmly established, there will be a persistent difficulty in learning higher order words. It may be necessary, even at secondary level, to fill the gaps in the child's core vocabulary.

The child who has *word retrieval problems* may have failed to understand the full meaning of the word.

This relies on an ability to recognise the relationship between words and concepts and their boundaries.

Word retrieval problems – difficulty accessing known vocabulary at will.

56

- **horse** – an animal you ride, but which is different from a donkey, a camel and an elephant.
- **horse** – a piece of gym equipment, linked through shape to the animal.
- **hoarse** – although sounding the same, is not part of the same concept.

Children who process slowly tend to pick out the words in a sentence which have a definite meaning and disregard the shorter, and apparently less important, words. As a result, they often totally misunderstand the sentence, failing to take account of words such as *prepositions* (e.g. behind, over), *conjunctions* (e.g. but, and, so) and *pronouns* (e.g. it, she, his).

Children are often able to predict word meaning from the context. When a child is struggling to understand a whole sentence, the context is easily lost and cannot, therefore, be used to support word meaning. *Homophones* (words which sound the same but have different meanings) rely entirely on context for their interpretation.

The language of feelings and emotions is harder to learn because it is non-concrete. The child must be able to empathise with the feeling in order to understand the concept and the associated vocabulary. Children functioning at the higher end of the autistic spectrum or those with a diagnosis of *semantic/pragmatic disorder* often find this very difficult.

Semantic/pragmatic disorder – a difficulty in interpreting the meanings of words or sentences (*semantics*) and in using them appropriately in context (*pragmatics*).

Do:

- **Be aware that there may be gaps in the core vocabulary.**
  If you suspect that a concept is not established, check that the child understands the words you have used in your explanation. Some words, which may seem to be very simple, may yet be misunderstood.

- **Write new vocabulary on the board and illustrate if possible.**
  This draws attention to the new word and helps to reinforce it.

- **Involve parents in learning new vocabulary.**
  Over-learning is essential in establishing new vocabulary concepts and this rehearsal and repetition can most easily and effectively be undertaken at home.

- **Back up more sophisticated vocabulary with simpler words.**
  In this way the child is introduced to new vocabulary in context and with explanation.

> **example**
>
> The glass is transparent, you can see through it.

- **Teach vocabulary using multi-sensory methods.**
  Use visual, auditory and practical clues to help establish new vocabulary.

- **Check understanding of more difficult vocabulary frequently.**
  Do not assume that the child has retained what you have previously taught him.

- **Use context to demonstrate new vocabulary.**
  This is more effective than teaching it in isolation.

- **Give appropriate vocabulary for homework in a word bank (a list of relevant words).**
  For example, in a task for expressive writing, the child can select words to use, which are not yet firmly established. This will also reinforce the meaning.

- **Use word derivations, whenever possible, when teaching new words.**
  Teaching word derivations helps the child's understanding of a specific word, as well as other related words.

---

example

microscope, telescope, horoscope.
'scope' = range
television, telecommunications, telescope, telepathic.
'tele' = at a distance

- **Write up word banks on the board.**
  By presenting the vocabulary relevant to the lesson, the burden of understanding is decreased and the words are reinforced.

- **Introduce new vocabulary slowly.**
  Establishing word meanings is time consuming and introducing too many at once is often confusing and counter-productive. It is important that the total concept of the word is fully established, if the child is to make use of it in more than one context. Children with language processing difficulties tend to compartmentalise information and are unable to transfer knowledge from one situation to another.

- Teach multiple meanings.

  The child may be confused when, having learnt the meaning of a word in one context, he then encounters it elsewhere with a different meaning.

> **example**
>
> 'Palm' as in hand and plant.
> 'Pound' as in money and beat.

- Be aware the child may misunderstand the implications of adverbs associated with many verbs. There is an obvious difference in meaning between take off, take away, take on, take through, etc. The child with weak processing, however, may fail to recognise the significance of such words.

Case study 1

Renard, aged 15, when told in a Science lesson to divide animals into their different categories of mammals, insects, birds, etc., was unable to do the task because he did not know what 'divide' meant in this context. He could undertake it as a Maths exercise but not Science.

Case study 2

Jack, aged 12, when told 'He was holding the wheel and put his foot on the brake.' thought that the person was riding a bike. He had heard 'wheel' and 'brake' and failed to process the less significant words in the sentence.

Resources

1 Anna Rhodes, *Rhodes to Language*. Stass Publications. ISBN 1-874534-31-4
2 Sadie Bigland and Jane Speake, *Semantic Links*. Stass Publications. ISBN 1-874534-02-0
3 Jane Speake and Sadie Bigland-Lewis, *Semantic Connections*. Stass Publications. ISBN 1-874534-14-4

Subject-specific vocabulary

Since some children have difficulty absorbing vocabulary in common usage, the problems of learning subject-specific vocabulary are magnified. These words must, therefore, be taught carefully, in a hierarchical structure, using the child's preferred mode of learning.

These are not words the child will have come across before, so he may have a preconceived notion that they are more difficult to learn. They are more likely to be encountered in a written rather than a spoken form and the child may not realise that the word he has read but mispronounced in his mind, is the same word as the one the teacher is saying.

Many of these words are multi-syllabic, with differences in meaning shown only by a single syllable, e.g. *hypoglycaemia/hyperglycaemia, carbon dioxide/carbon monoxide, pentagon/hexagon.*

The child's weak vocabulary affects his ability to recognise word derivations, e.g. *bicuspid, biennial, bilateral, bilingual, binocular, bivalve,* and some words, which are familiar, have a changed meaning, e.g. *plates, cell, table, field, reaction, resistance, power.*

Do:

- **Discover the child's preferred mode of learning.**
  Multi-sensory teaching is essential in teaching these complex words. It is important to know which sensory channel the child responds to most readily.

- **Make multi-sensory associations when teaching vocabulary.**
  Techniques such as mnemonics, cartoon pictures, rhyming, humour and colour help to establish the vocabulary in long-term memory.

- **Encourage the child to make his own associations wherever possible.**
  If the child 'owns' the idea then he is more likely to remember it.

- **Encourage children to share their ideas.**
  The child who is weaker in thinking up associations may be supported by a more imaginative member of the class.

- **Write the word as you are explaining it and use practical demonstrations as well.**
  It is important that the child clearly understands the context of the vocabulary, correct pronunciation of the word and its written form.

- **Predict words which might be in common usage and use this as a link to the new meaning.**
  If the child already knows a meaning of the word, link it to the scientific one.

example

Cell – the idea of a prisoner isolated in a cell may help the child understand the scientific meaning of cell.

- **Make associations with real life experiences.**
  The child with language difficulties may be unable to relate what he learns in the classroom to real life and may need to have his attention drawn to it very specifically.

- **Ensure that the structure of new vocabulary is fully explained.**
  The child is more likely to remember and understand the word if he is able to make associations between it and known vocabulary. An explanation of the word's derivation and its similarity in meaning to other words, helps to anchor it in the child's memory .

- **Ensure that basic concept words are known before teaching higher order vocabulary.**
  There is a danger in assuming that the child understands the simpler concepts, on which to base new knowledge. For example, unless the child has some understanding of energy, he will not be able to grasp the concept of renewable sources.

Case study 1

Richard, aged 19 and an undergraduate at university, had particular difficulty with the pharmacology vocabulary. Although he recognised the patterns of the written words, he had not internalised their pronunciation correctly and, therefore, did not realise that they were the same words as the ones he had heard in the lecture.

Case study 2

Kurt, aged 15, was unable to recall the parts of the eye, until he thought up the following sentence: Lens daughter Iris, who was a pupil at the school on the cornea retina café next to the optician. (Len's daughter Iris, who was a pupil at the school on the corner, ate in a café next to the optician.)

Resources

1   Wendy Rinaldi, *Language Concepts to Access Learning*. 18 Dorking Road, Chilworth, Surrey GV4 8NR.

Word Cog 1

Level 1

Select an item and describe it according to all the given categories. These can be as extensive as desired. For instance 'Where do you find it?' could be as many situations as the child can think of. Also, the 'Description' could be as detailed as the child is able to give.

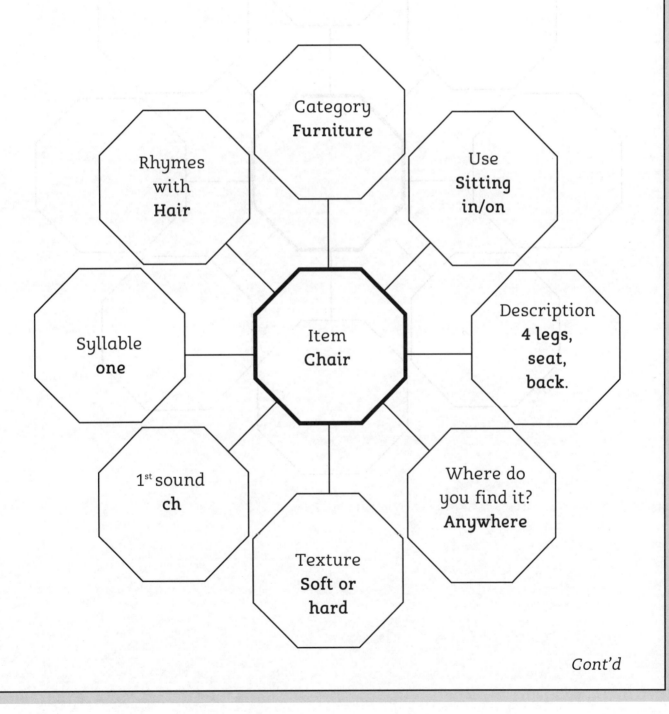

Cont'd

Word cog 1

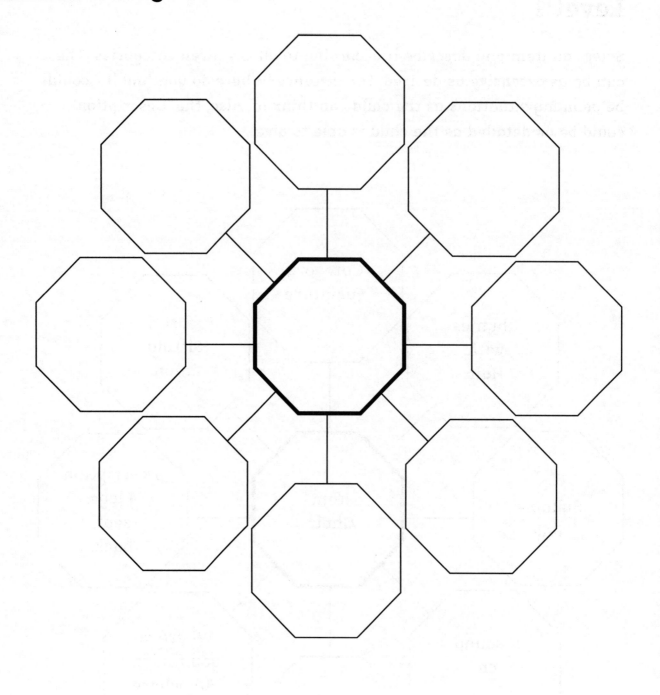

Word Cog 2

Level 2

Complete Level 1 and then think of three other items to fill in each section of outer level.

Example

- **Category:** tools – Saw, nail, spirit level.
- **Texture:** hard, metallic, smooth – car, iron, cooker.
- **Ist sound:** p – parrot, problem, possibility.

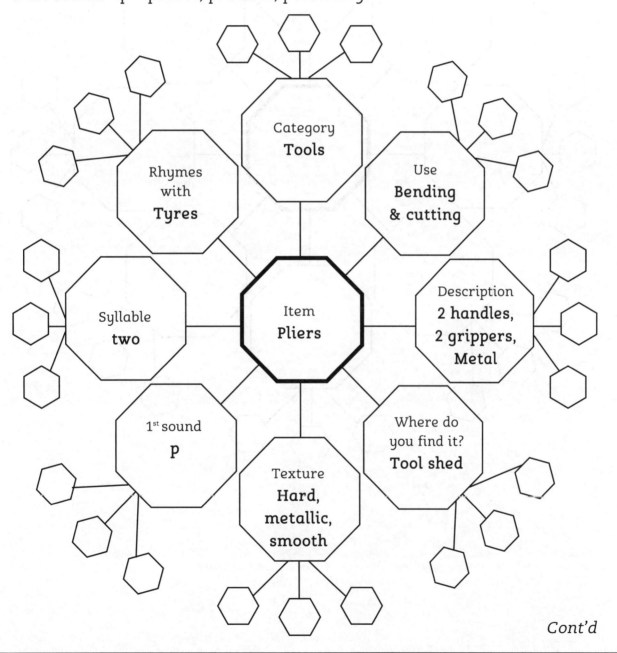

Cont'd

Word cog 2

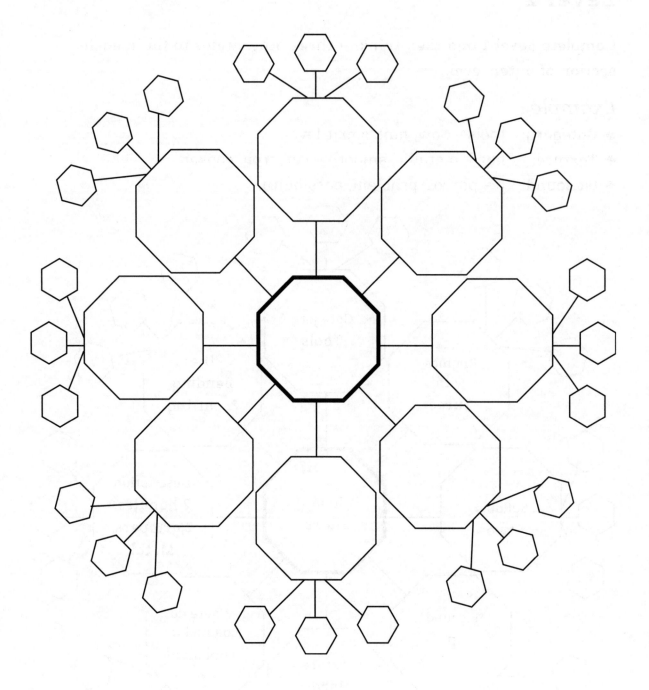

Developing Vocabulary

Examples of how to develop vocabulary

Main category: ANIMALS

Sub-categories, showing cross references:

Pets (P)	dogs (Fm), cats, gerbils, rabbits (WA), tortoises (Z), horses (Fm), goldfish (F)
Farm (Fm)	cows, sheep, pigs, dogs (P), chickens (B), geese (B), goats (H), turkeys (B)
Birds (B)	bluetit, thrush, turkey (Fm), chicken (Fm), duck (Fm), eagle
Fish (F)	cod, carp, goldfish (P), pike, shark (C), octopus
Insect (I)	bee, ant, grasshopper, mosquito, ladybird, wasp
Wild (British) animals (WA)	hedgehog, deer (H), fox (C), rabbit (P, H), stoat (C)
Zoo (Z)	lion (C), tiger (C), tortoise (P, H), giraffe, wildebeest, monkey, buffalo, parrot (B)
Carnivore (C)	dog (P, Fm), lion (Z), wasp (I)
Herbivore (H)	cow (Fm), sheep (Fm), wildebeest (Z)

Cont'd

Enlarging on a sub-category:

Farm animals

Cows	*Produce:*
	Meat – beef, steak, mince, beef-burgers, stews
	Milk – cheese, butter, yoghurt, cream, clotted cream, ice cream
	Leather – shoes, belts, wallets, handbags
	Young – calves

Pigs, sheep, chickens, turkeys, ducks, horses, etc. expanded in the same way.

Other areas to explore:

Why we keep animals

Meat	cows, sheep, pigs
Company	dogs, cats, goldfish, budgies
Transport	horse, bullock, donkey, camel
Sport	horses, hounds, ferrets, beagles, greyhounds
Business	wool, leather, feathers

Why we protect animals

Interest	birdwatching, safari, snorkelling
Conservation	endangered species, preventing over-fishing, pollination
Love of animals	stray dogs, cats, garden birds

Animal food chains

worm → blackbird → cat

greenfly → ladybird → bluetit → sparrowhawk

grass → zebra → lion

Animal-specific vocabulary

Riding	hoof, mane, tail, halter, horseshoe, bridle, saddle, girth, reins
Fishing	rod, line, fly, coarse, fin, scale
Elephant	trunk, tusk, bull, cow

Cont'd

 © M Davenport & P Hall 2004   Listening and Understanding in Secondary Schools   5 Vocabulary

Word web

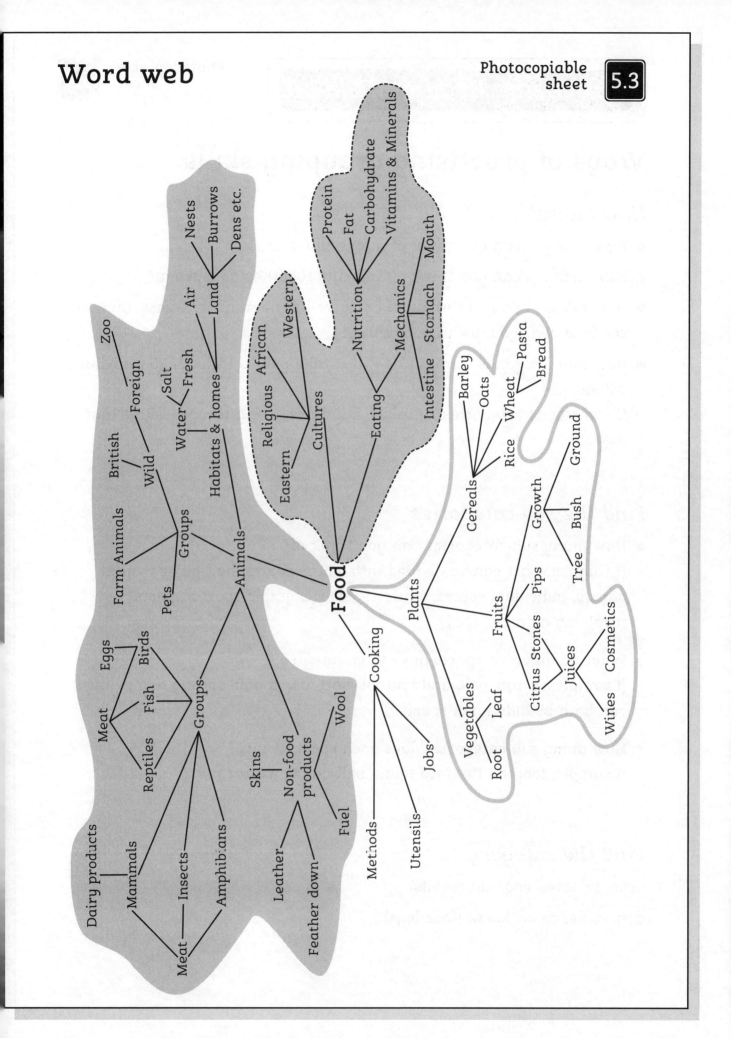

Ways of practising grouping skills

How many?

● How many … can you think of in one minute?

● How many … can you think of, working together as a group?

● How many … do you think you can give in one minute? Guess, and then see how near you are to your target.

● How many seconds or minutes will it take you to think of 20 items in a category?
(Examples of categories: animals, buildings, living things, things that move.)

Find the sub-categories

● **How many sub-categories can you think of?**
(Example: sport can be divided into water sports, ball games, team games, individual sports, winter sports, Olympic sports, sports involving animals, etc.)

● **What do different sports have in common?**
(Examples: water polo and football both use a ball, sailing and riding can both be individual sports.)

● **How many sub-categories does each sport fit into?**
(Example: football fits into team, ball game, winter.)

Find the category

crab, tortoise, egg, nut (**shells**)

dog, table, chair, horse (**four legs**)

Find the odd one out

Train, *boat*, car, van, airplane (**wheels**)

Australia, *Europe*, India, Canada (**countries**)

Sorting into categories

Using pictures:

- Sort them into categories.

- Put two pictures out and ask the child to pick a third one that fits the category.

- Take two random pictures and ask for one difference and one similarity.

Alternative categories

- What categories could ... belong in?
  (e.g. chair could be furniture, wooden, school, relaxation)

Word association

Go round in a circle, each child giving a word that he associates with the previous word. If challenged, he must defend his choice.

(e.g. ball—tennis—lawn—material—wood—chair)

More ways of practising grouping skills

Opposites
Give a word that means the opposite of:

hot	front	good	dry
deep	narrow	clean	day
adult	right	buy	old
bright	early	polite	rich
liquid	public	exit	float
multiply	rapid	noise	clever
vacant	hollow	empty	question

Same meaning
Give a word that means the same as:

sad	noisy	round	look
gap	small	escape	new
feeble	hello	rough	conceal
transparent	complicated	international	peculiar
comprehend	enormous	least	astonish
sign	surrounded	famous	option
trick	commence	loving	exterior

Same sound but different meaning

Give the different meanings of:

pear/pair/pare	meet/meat	blue/blew
hair/hare	hear/here	bare/bear
plain/plane	stationary/stationery	leek/leak
steak/stake	break/brake	hoard/horde
hole/whole	wait/weight	board/bored
grown/groan	wood/would	their/there
ceiling/sealing	council/counsel	muscle/mussel
peace/piece	medal/meddle	scene/seen
reign/rain/rein	draft/draught	throne/thrown

TARGET

Name: —————— Date: ——————

Use your word bank!

TARGET

Name: —————— Date: ——————

Do you understand the word? Ask.

Word   Meaning

1 ————   ————
2 ————   ————
3 ————   ————
4 ————   ————

TARGET

Name: —————— Date: ——————

Learn 5 new words.

Word   Meaning

1 ————   ————
2 ————   ————
3 ————   ————
4 ————   ————
5 ————   ————

TARGET

Name: —————— Date: ——————

Find another word instead of:

1 nice   ————
2 good   ————
3 said   ————
4 thing ————

TARGET

Name: _____ Date: _____

Teach a friend your method of remembering.

What is your method?

TARGET

Name: _____ Date: _____

Learn 5 new subject words.

Word   Meaning

1 ____   ____
2 ____   ____
3 ____   ____
4 ____   ____
5 ____   ____

TARGET

Name: _____ Date: _____

Make up a way to remember the word and its meaning.

TARGET

Name: _____ Date: _____

Make up a mnemonic for learning a sequence.

The Concept of Time

Time is a basic life skill and one which is frequently misunderstood by children with language processing difficulties. Both calendar and time-telling are intangible concepts represented in many different ways, such as diaries, timetables, analogue and digital clocks, time-lines and programmes.

Children are expected to follow several different presentations of time in the classroom. The timetable is a grid, homework diaries are vertical, calendars are often horizontal, the classroom clock is probably analogue and therefore circular, while the child's watch may be digital. It is possible, however, to demonstrate time in a consistently linear way, which will help to clarify the child's understanding.

The understanding of time relies on logical sequencing, which is a weakness for many children with specific learning difficulties. If the child has no idea of the order of his day, the length of a week or the duration of a term, he will be unable to organise appointments, homework deadlines and revision schedules.

The secondary school child, who still has difficulty telling the time, needs to learn digital time but on an analogue clock face. Analogue time, which goes, for instance, from '25 past', to 'half past', to '25 to', is very confusing for the child with sequencing difficulties. He has to be able to count in two different directions, and understand both the prepositions *past* and *to*, as well as the fractions *quarter* and *half*. Digital time uses a more logical sequence but, since analogue clocks are commonplace, the inability to use them puts the child at a disadvantage. It is also possible for him to read the time from a digital watch without having any real understanding of the concept. Another reason for learning digital time is that it is a common feature in daily life, such as in television programme schedules and in timetables for schools, buses and trains.

The child who does not appreciate the difference between an hour and a minute, is unable to plan his day adequately. He will frequently be late because he cannot work out where he should be and has to rely on following others. He will not appreciate when he has to hurry or when he still has time available.

Time vocabulary is extremely wide and varied and it cannot be assumed that children have a proper understanding of even the most commonly used terms.

For example:

- **Clock**: seconds, minutes, hours.
- **Day**: morning, dawn, lunchtime.
- **Calendar**: months, seasons, terms, holidays.
- **Sequential**: before, after, last, the last, next, future.
- **Phrases**: two weeks time, for two weeks, two weeks ago.

Memory and time are inextricably linked. Unless the child understands time, he has no formal structure in which to store memories of events, so is then unable to recall them.

History teaching should be child-centred. While many children enjoy learning about ancient history and benefit from it, it means very little to them in historical terms. Starting with the present day and working chronologically backwards helps to teach the concept of elapsed time. Children learn more readily when they are able to relate their knowledge to the experiences of their parents and grandparents.

Do:

- **Write the date on the board using the name of the month rather than the number.**
  This will reinforce the naming and sequence of the months. Using the number only may teach the child that it is the sixth month but not that it is called June.

- **Make a linear calendar for classroom use.**
  The child who has problems with time concepts will find it easier to understand the concept of a year, if the calendar is in one continuous line, divided into seasons, terms, months, weeks and days. This calendar should be referred to for all time-based activities.

- **Make children aware of deadlines, using a linear calendar.**
  Telling the child to give in a piece of work 'in two weeks time' may not mean anything to him. Seeing it on the calendar in relation to other events helps him organise his time.

- **Be aware of possible difficulties with temporal/sequential time language.**
  It is surprising how many children in secondary school confuse the meaning of 'before' and 'after', for example.

- **Refer to the clock regularly during the lesson.**
  Give an overview of the length of the lesson and how it will be divided into different activities. This may be the first time that the child is given the experience of what 10 minutes or 30 minutes feel like.

- **Relate time keeping to concrete events.**
  Understanding time is made easier if it is linked to the child's experience, such as the length of a lesson, duration of favourite TV programmes, or the journey time to school.

- **Teach time vocabulary.**
  Many children do not understand the meaning of words such as *term*, *break up*, *holiday*, *season*, *decade*, *century*, *annual*.

- **Teach digital time using an analogue clock.**
  This reinforces the understanding of time as a logical sequence, with the counting following the movement of the hands in a continual, clockwise direction. Having to count back anticlockwise (as in 20 to 9) can be confusing. It also avoids the difficulty of when to use 'past' and 'to'.

- **Relate the teaching of history to the child's family context.**
  Encouraging children to talk to their relations about their experiences in life makes history more real to them.

- **Make use of a history time line.**
  Children who have difficulty in understanding time concepts need to have 'anchors' around which to relate historical events.

Case study 1

Pat, aged 13, when asked the date, replied 'The third of the sixth, two thousand and three.' She had no idea of the name of the month, although she did know that the school broke up in July. This meant that she could not work out how long it was until the end of term.

Case study 2

Nick, aged 15, was fascinated by the story of the *Marie Celeste*. When asked when he thought it took place, he replied 'Oh, I think it was BC.'

Helping the child to understand the calendar

Many children with language processing difficulties do not understand calendar time. They cannot 'see' a year, a month or a week, and so have only a hazy impression of the words we all use to organise our time, such as **seasons, months, terms, holidays, fortnight, half-term.**

Some of the expressions related to calendar time are particularly confusing because of their similarity. For example: **last month, the month before last, the last month.**

- How long was your holiday?
- How long ago was your holiday?
- How many weeks till your holiday?
- How many weeks was your holiday?

A linear calendar, which allows the child to view the whole year at a time, enables him to see the different ways in which a year may be divided, e.g. **months, seasons, terms** and **holidays.** (See demonstration calendar for January and February.)

Seasons should be printed on different coloured paper (e.g. grey/white for winter, green for spring, yellow for summer and orange/brown for autumn), terms and holidays should be indicated and weekend dates shown in red, to help when counting by weeks. The calendar can be personalised as the year progresses by marking birthdays, special days, outings, regular events such as school clubs, and infrequent events such as family holidays.

It can be used to see how long a term or a holiday may be, or how long until a birthday or Christmas.

Cont'd

When teaching calendar time, it is more useful for the child, initially, to be able to find his way around the calendar, and to use it as a tool in everyday life, rather than being expected to learn all the calendar terms by heart. Some children, for example, may know the months in sequence, but not know the name of the current month, or how long a month is.

Always start with **NOW**. Find the month and the day. Establish which season it is, which term, etc. Talk about last month or next month, but try to keep in the here and now.

Establish, pointing to the calendar and counting, that in each year there are:

● 12 months

● 4 seasons

● 3 terms

● 3 school holidays

● 1 birthday for each person

Relate every calendar-based fact back to the teaching calendar. Children are always interested in when things are going to happen, e.g. school outings, visits to the dentist, end of term (many children do not know what a term is, and do not understand when someone asks when they 'break up'), Christmas, Hallowe'en, November 5th, etc.

Using the calendar as an everyday tool will help the child assimilate an idea of time without realising he is doing so.

Demonstration calendar

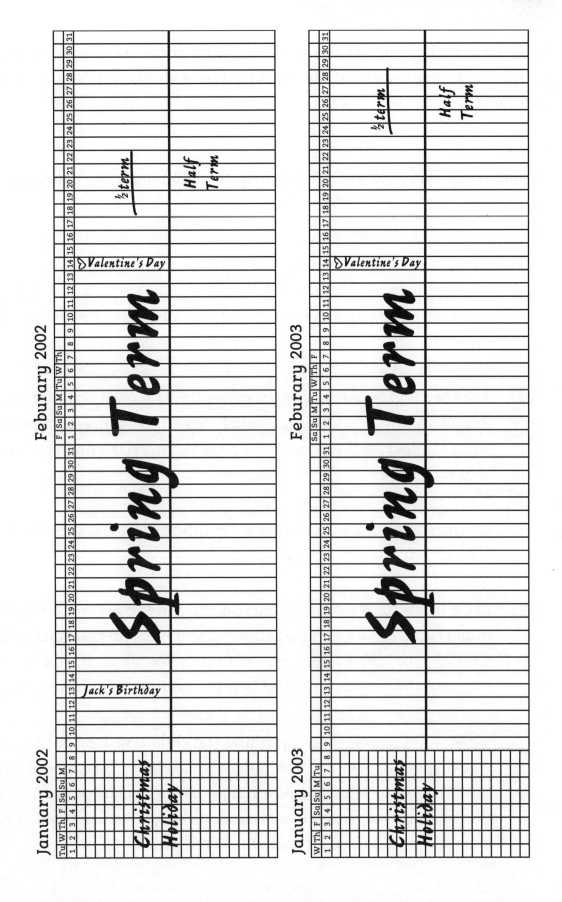

Time Management

Until the child has a conscious understanding of the passage of time, he will find it difficult to recall the representative words (e.g. minute, hour, fortnight).

The following exercises are used to help the child link time concepts and words.

1 Count out, with the child, 60 seconds to make one minute. Practise the speed necessary for accuracy, then ask the child to close his eyes and put up his hand when he thinks one minute is up.

2 Ask the child to estimate how many times he can complete a task in one minute, e.g. write his name, repeat his address, or walk from his desk to the door. Then time the exercise and see how accurate he is.

   Do the same sort of exercises with different times, such as 15 seconds, 30 seconds or 2 minutes.

3 Set a timer for 5 minutes, and ask the child to estimate how many sums he can complete, how many lines he can read in that time or how long he can concentrate and work on his own. Increase the times to 10 minutes, 15 minutes, 20 minutes, etc.

4 Reverse these exercises by asking the child how long he has been working on an activity, how long a lesson lasts, how long it takes him to cycle to school or how long it takes to change for a games lesson. In each case, give him three alternatives from which to choose. For example, 10 seconds, 10 minutes or 10 hours.

Cont'd

5   At the start of the lesson, point out the time. Tell the child how
    long the lesson will last, and, using a teaching clock, set the hands
    to show when the lesson will end. Calculate how long the lesson
    will last. Stop several times during the lesson to see how much
    time has passed and how long there is till the lesson ends. This is
    often the first time that the child begins to understand how to
    relate passing time to the hands on the clock.

6   When setting a deadline for homework or course work, help the
    child to draw out a linear chart, marking the days or weeks, so
    that he can colour in or put a cross against the time as the
    deadline approaches.

7   Discuss with the child how long it takes to complete a piece of
    work and relate this to a time experience familiar to him. For
    example, knowing that a favourite television programme lasts 30
    minutes will give him some idea of what he is expected to do in
    30 minutes.

8   Make a 24-hour day chart to help the child to compare lengths of
    time. Using this he will be able to compare how long it takes to
    get to school with the length of a lesson, or the time taken for
    lunch with the length of time expected for homework.

Time Vocabulary

Daily

Morning
Afternoon
Evening
Night
Dawn
Daybreak
Noon
Midday
Twilight
Dusk
Midnight
Sunrise
Sunset
Breakfast time
Dinnertime
Lunchtime
Teatime
Suppertime
Early morning
Early evening
Mid-afternoon
Late afternoon
Late at night
Yesterday
Tomorrow
Day before yesterday
Day after tomorrow
Second
Minute
Hour
Half hour
Quarter of an hour
Three quarters of an hour
5 minutes
10 minutes/seconds
12 hours
24 hours
Birthday

Annual

Month
Season
Spring
Summer
Autumn
Winter
Term
Half-term
1st/2nd half of term
Bank holiday
Week
Fortnight
Holiday
Holidays
Break up
Easter
Christmas
New Year
Hallowe'en
Bonfire night
St.Valentine's day
Boxing Day
Leap year
Decade
Century
Centenary
Millennium
Annual
Bi-annual
Perennial
Next week
The next week/month
Last week/month
In 2 weeks time
For 2 weeks
2 weeks until
2 weeks ago
Week after next

Sequential

Next
The next
Last
The last
2nd from last
Last but one
After
Before
Between
From
First
Penultimate
While
Until
Soon
Nearly
Almost
Then
When
Which day?

1 | Mary took her three year old child to school.
Is Mary: 10   30   60 years old?

2 | John got up early to do the milk round.
Is it: dawn   noon   dusk?

3 | Mrs. Andrews went to collect her pension.
Is she: 25   45   65 years old?

4 | The swallows arrived from Africa.
Is it: winter   spring   autumn?

5 | The scout group celebrated their centenary.
Is the group: 25   50   100 years old?

6 | Mr Brown returned to England after a decade abroad.
Had he been away for: 2   5   10   25 years?

7 | George was still too young to drive a car.
Is he: 16   18   20 years old?

8 | After his birthday on August 18th, Tom looked forward to Christmas.
Did he have to wait: 2   4   6 months?

9 | Jane ran down the stairs at home.
Did it take: 5 secs   1min   5 mins?

10 | Sam knew he would be half an hour late for the evening meeting at 6.
Did he arrive at: 6.30 a.m.   6.30 p.m.   5.30 p.m.?

How long do I have to complete the exercises?

Name: _____ Date: _____

5 mins ——	30 mins ——
10 mins ——	40 mins ——
15 mins ——	45 mins ——
20 mins ——	50 mins ——

1 hour ——
1 day ——
1 week ——
1 month ——

How many days until the coursework must be handed in?

Name: _____ Date: _____

14	13	12	11	10	9	8
7	6	5	4	3	2	1

How long is this lesson?

Name: _____ Date: _____

30 minutes ☐   **1 hour** ☐

What is the date today?

Name: _____ Date: _____

Day:

Date:

Month:

Year:

Whole Date:

© M Davenport & P Hall 2004   Listening and Understanding in Secondary Schools   6 The Concept of Time

Spatial Concepts

The language issues associated with spatial concepts encompass the understanding of the world and its divisions, the child's personal environment and spatial vocabulary.

Some children, though they may be able to recite their address, have no understanding of its significance. They may not appreciate that each line of the address signifies a different concept, sequenced logically from the specific to the general. Such children do not know that houses have names or numbers, that these numbers relate to the position in the street or road, that the road is part of a larger community called a village or town and that this, in turn, is part of a county.

This confusion is often reflected in a difficulty in understanding the world and its boundaries. While these children may be aware that there are many countries in the world and that they live in Great Britain, they do not have an overview of the world and, therefore, cannot relate their information to the world map. This has obvious implications for teaching geography.

The concepts associated with the vocabulary such as street, town, county, country, continent are often poorly understood. It is not uncommon for a child to believe that the town he lives in is in fact a country, or that, despite the number of his house being 82, there are only a few houses in his street. The use of these terms, therefore, does not enable the child to infer information about relative size and importance.

Other difficulties with spatial vocabulary include prepositional words and phrases, such as 'between', 'in the middle of', 'behind', points of the compass and measurement and orientation, such as left/right, horizontal/vertical, latitude/longitude.

Do:

- **Check every child knows his address and understands it.**
  Understanding a simplified postal delivery system helps the child to make sense of his address.

- **Make sure every child knows his own left/right, or has some easy way to sort this out.**
  Children may have difficulty with left/right orientation. Even if this is not a problem, higher order concepts such as the difference between 'to the left of' and 'on his left' may cause confusion.

- **Make sure the child understands terms related to direction.**
  Commonly used phrases such as 'round the next bend', 'at the crossroads', 'just before', 'between', etc. are often misunderstood.

- **Make sure points of the compass are understood.**
  When teaching points of the compass, relate the information to places familiar to the child.

- **Use a map of the world to mark places of personal and/or national interest.**
  Children build up their knowledge of the world by collating information from many different sources, e.g. holidays, news items, relatives living abroad, postcards, lessons, advertisements.

- Do check that the child understands commonly used prepositions.

    Interpreting terms such as 'in front of', 'beside' and 'between' depends on your perspective and may be different for a person in another position.

Case study 1

Dan, aged 12, knew the names of all the teams playing in the World Cup and their continents. However, when asked to find them on the map, he had no idea what the word 'continent' implied, so was unable to find the countries, or understand that, having located one European country, another would be close by.

Case study 2

Ann, aged 11, thought that she lived in the town of Great Portland Street, in the country of London.

Name: _____

Address: _____

_____

_____

Surname: _____

First names(s): _____

Address: House name/number _____

Street name _____

Town _____

County _____

Postcode _____

Telephone: _____ _____

Title: Mr/Mrs/Miss/Ms/Other _____

Initials: _____

Surname: _____

Address: _____

_____

_____

Postcode: _____

Bus Queue Questions

Left/right, sequencing, orientation and negatives.
(Point to the answers in the picture of a bus queue on the next page.)

1 Who is on the right of the girl drinking out of the bottle?

2 Who is behind the lady with a bag over her left shoulder?

3 How many people are holding things in their right hands?

4 What is the old lady holding in her left hand?

5 Which lady has a bag over her left shoulder?

6 Which girl is holding a bottle in her right hand?

7 Who is to the right of the man holding a rolled-up newspaper?

8 Is the man holding a newspaper on the right or the left of the man reading a newspaper?

9 Who is probably left handed?

10 How many people are there to the left of the old lady?

11 Who is to the right of the lady with spiky hair, and to the left of the lady carrying 3 bags?

12 What is the man with long hair holding in his right hand?

13 How many people are facing left?

14 Who is first in the queue?

15 Who is second from last in the queue?

16 Who is fourth in the queue?

17 Who in the queue is in front of the boy sitting on the pavement?

18 Who is facing the plump old lady?

19 Who is between the old lady and the little boy?

20 Who is next to the girl with a ponytail?

21 Who has her back to the old lady?

22 Who is next but one to the man with glasses?

23 Who will be sixth onto the bus?

24 Who do you know has an earring in their left ear?

25 Who has most of their weight on their left leg?

26 Who is not standing between 2 people?

27 Whose bag is on the ground to his right?

28 Who is not holding anything in their left hand?

29 Who is not facing the front of the queue?

30 Who is not standing up?

Bus queue

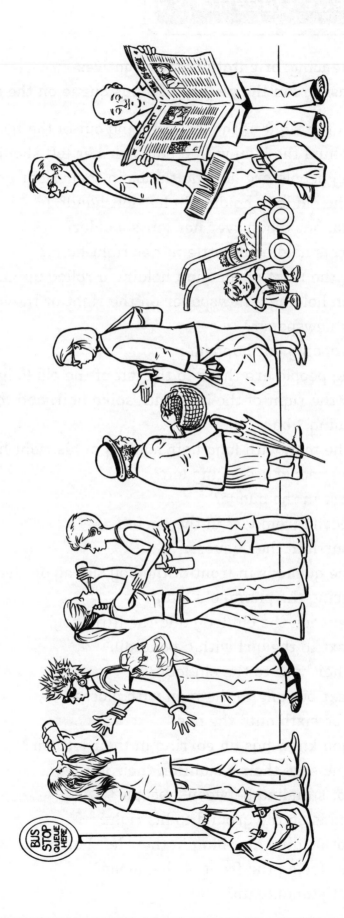

Map Directions

These directions can be given as the child studies the map on the next sheet, or, to make this exercise more realistic and useful, by giving the child the instruction before he sees the map. It is, however, important to help the child to succeed by breaking down each instruction and helping him to visualise what you are saying.

(The answers are given at the end of each instruction.)

1. Start at the station. Drive to the roundabout and take the road going North East. Where will you end up? *(New Town)*

2. Start at X on the map. Drive over the river till you come to a crossroads, then turn due North. Where will you be? *(Station)*

3. Start at Y on the map, cross the level crossing, and at the crossroads turn West. Take the next left. In which direction are you facing, and if you carry on along that road, in which direction will you then be going? *(SW NW)*

4. Starting in the town, go to the roundabout, go East and then turn right. Which way are you facing? *(S)*

5. Start at X, go under the railway bridge, straight over the crossroads, take the first left, then the next right. What are you driving past? *(Pond)*

6. You have to wait because a train is coming, and you are facing North. Take the second left and then left again. Where might you have to stop? *(Traffic Lights)*

7. From the station, take the second on the right, first left and then first right. What is on your left as you make this last turning? *(Bench)*

8. Start at Y and go over the level crossing. Take the first right, then second left. Go straight over the crossroads. What is on your right? *(Church)*

9. Which direction is the town from the station? *(E)*

10. From the town, go across the roundabout, take the first left, then the second left and you will come to your house. Which is it? *(W)*

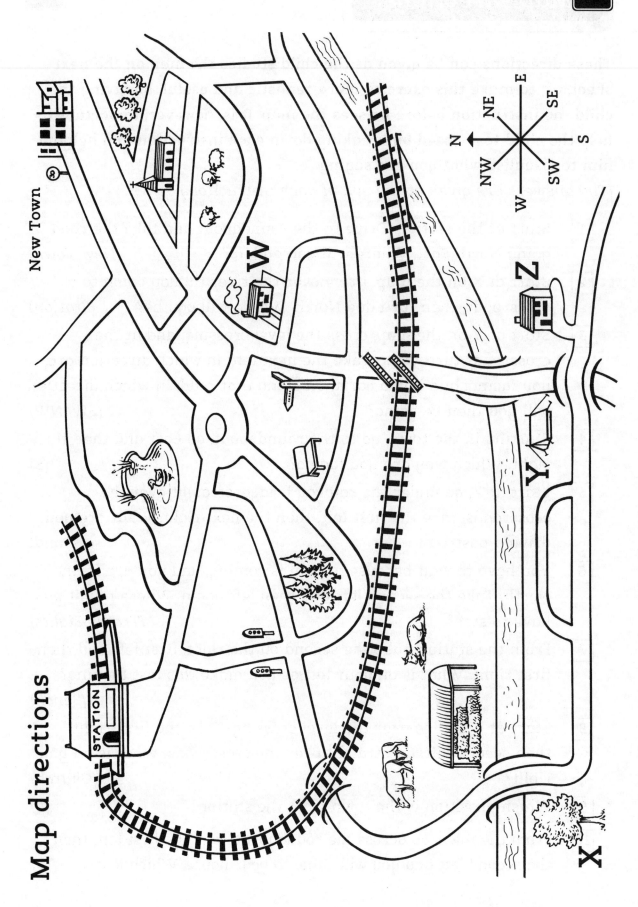

Map directions

New Town

STATION

W

Z

Y

X

N · NE · E
NW · · SE
W · SW · S

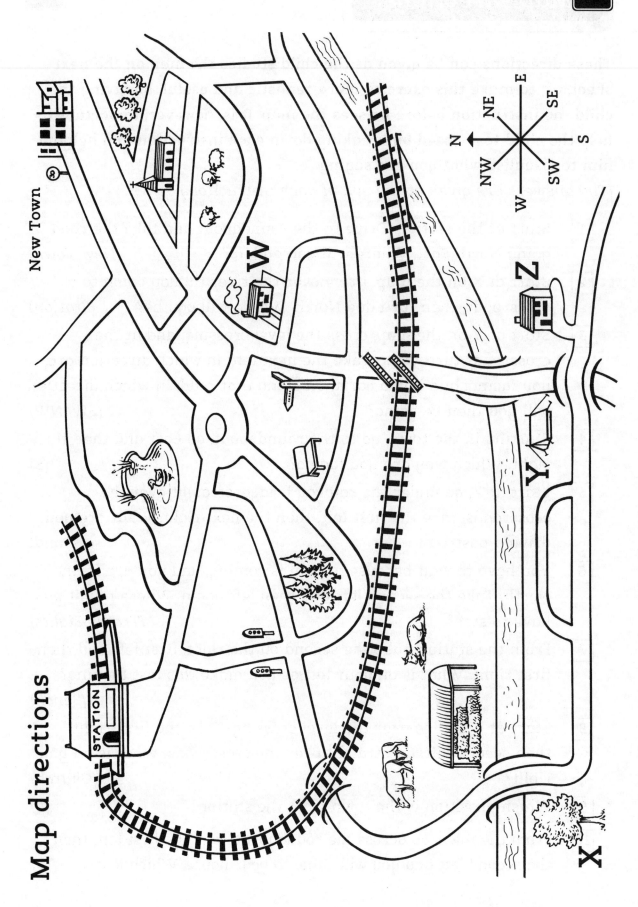

Travel Plans

You want to travel from home to the following places. What means of transport would you take and how long do you think it would take you?

1   To school.

2   To Edinburgh.

3   To the cinema.

4   To Oxford Circus in the centre of London.

5   To the local supermarket.

6   To the leisure centre.

7   To Sydney, Australia.

8   To Land's End.

9   To New York.

10   To Disneyland, Paris.

11   To visit your grandmother.

12   A holiday in the Sahara Desert.

13   A holiday in the West Indies.

14   To Alton Towers.

15   A Mediterranean cruise.

16   To the Isle of Skye.

17   To the Isle of Wight.

18   To the Seychelles.

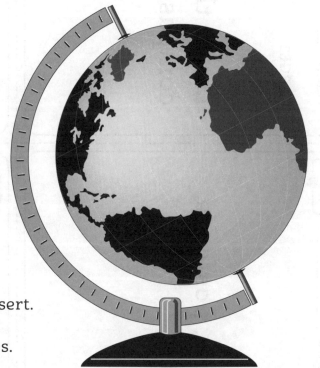

TARGET

Name: _____ Date: _____

Learn your address, postcode and phone number.

TARGET

Name: _____ Date: _____

Learn the points of the compass.

TARGET

Name: _____ Date: _____

Learn 5 major cities in the UK and where they are.

Bristol: _____

London: _____

Edinburgh: _____

Cardiff: _____

Birmingham: _____

TARGET

Name: _____ Date: _____

Learn the continents of the world.

Europe   Asia

North America   Australasia

South America   Antarctica

Africa

Figurative and Non-concrete Language

Figurative language includes concepts such as *idioms*, *analogies*, *metaphors* and the language of *humour*.

> **Idiom** – a saying that should not be translated literally, e.g. *to kill two birds with one stone*.
>
> **Analogy** – using a comparison to explain meaning, e.g. *likening the heart to a pump*.
>
> **Metaphor** – enhancing meaning by describing something in a non-literal way, e.g. *the horse flew across the field*.
>
> **Similie** – describing one thing in comparison to another, using 'as' or 'like', e.g. *he sang like a bird; he sat as still as a stone*.

As children's language develops, they recognise that what is said should not always be interpreted literally, although they may not yet understand the intended meaning.

The child who fails to understand idioms is easily confused when they are used. Unless he realises that 'pull your socks up' is a figure of speech, his probable response may be seen as facetious or belligerent. Similarly, when hearing metaphors and analogies, he may only understand the literal meaning and be unable to consider other interpretations. *Sarcasm* and *irony* may also be considered as figurative language, since what is said should not be translated literally. Sarcasm relies on the child recognising the tone of voice, and irony on realising that the actual words used are the opposite of what is meant.

Much of children's social interaction relies on the use of colloquial language, jokes and puns. The child who cannot cope with these aspects of language is in danger of becoming socially isolated.

Non-concrete language encompasses words and concepts which cannot be represented either literally or visually. They include words of feelings and emotion, such as sorrow, anger and bravery, which are widely used in the secondary curriculum.

Do:

- **Make a list of idioms you use.**
  These are much more commonly used than is often realised. Monitoring your own idiomatic language can alert you to the problems the child may have in understanding.

- **Teach the meanings of the idioms that you commonly use.**
  The child will learn the ones heard in the classroom more readily than random examples.

- **Be aware that idioms may be interpreted literally.**
  There is a danger of thinking that a child is being unco-operative, when in fact he is following your instruction to the best of his ability.

- **Use sarcasm and irony with caution.**
  While many children appreciate sarcasm and irony, those with language difficulties find it confusing and unsettling.

- **Be aware that the child may incorporate his literal interpretation of a metaphor into his understanding.**

From the phrase 'in the fox-red fallen leaves' it is possible for the child to believe that the story is about a fox.

- **Be aware of the child who laughs at jokes he does not understand.**
  He may be laughing at jokes in order to be accepted by his peers. This is often the first sign of social isolation.

- **Teach words of emotion and feelings.**
  Until the child is familiar with such vocabulary, he will find it very difficult to understand or express his own emotions. He may use other ways of venting his feelings, such as through physical behaviour.

- **Use word banks to show the variety of vocabulary that can be used to convey shades of emotion.**
  The child with weak vocabulary is inclined only to use emotion words at the extremes of the spectrum, such as: happy/sad, happy/angry.

Case study 1

Alex, aged 11, when called 'a goody-two-shoes' by her peers, said to the teacher 'I don't understand why they call me that ... what's wrong with having two shoes?'.

Case study 2

Tom, aged 13, used the word 'sad' to describe how he felt both when his grandfather died and when he discovered that fish and chips was off the lunch menu.

Resources

1   Sharon G. Webber, *Idioms Fun Deck*. Super Duper Publications (Taskmaster).

2   Tony Mitchell, *Photo Feelings Fun Deck*. Super Duper Publications (Taskmaster).

3   John Arena, *Idioms Delight*. High Noon Books. ISBN 0-87879-889-7

4   Photo Emotions, supplied by LDA

5   *Get the Joke*, Books 1, 2 and 3. Cutting Edge Publications, Pill House Farm, Lostwithiel, Cornwall PL22 0JR.

6   Joke books.

Word Bank

Feelings and emotions

happy	unhappy	serious
contented	irritated	timid
pleased	annoyed	afraid
cheerful	furious	ashamed
amused	angry	bored
gentle	ill-tempered	confused
brave	aggressive	disappointed
careful	impatient	embarrassed
considerate	lazy	exasperated
thoughtful	sad	frustrated
tolerant	frightened	strict
patient	wary	rude
sensitive	suspicious	obstinate
relaxed	greedy	moody
optimistic	hungry	immature
kind	desperate	eccentric
jovial	cruel	timid
enthusiastic	vague	courageous
creative	sulky	pensive
sensible	worried	interested
clever	stupid	amusing
confident	anxious	perceptive
curious	careless	grumpy
ambitious	insolent	gloomy
sympathetic	impudent	excitable
intelligent	intolerant	idle
energetic	impatient	apathetic
calm	stubborn	inconsiderate
peaceful	sarcastic	modest
content	pompous	melancholy
conventional	pessimistic	diligent

John looked in dismay at the piles of old clothes at the jumble sale. There were at least 10 tables full of them, how was he going to find Grandad's favourite tie? It was like looking for a needle in a haystack.

What does 'looking for a needle in a haystack' mean?

Joe and his dad stood side by side in front of Mrs Jones. They both had round red faces, spiky orange hair and sticky-out ears. 'Well,' she said, smiling at them, 'he's a chip off the old block, isn't he?'

What does 'chip off the old block' mean?

Nick's dad was trying to sell their old car. The man who wanted to buy it was suggesting that he should take the car away with him, and post a cheque to Nick's dad the next day. 'Oh no,' said Nick's dad, shaking his head, 'that won't do, I want the money up front.'

What does 'up front' mean?

'Quick, Quick,' screamed Lisa out of the window, as Darren opened the gate. 'Grandad's bought you a ...' Dad slammed the window shut. 'Stop, Lisa,' he said, 'you know Grandad wants it to be a surprise. You nearly let the cat out of the bag.'

What does it mean to 'let the cat out of the bag'?

Old Mr Burt spread the money out in front of them on the table. They needed £40 for the rent, £6 for the electricity bill and £7 for the gas bill. Then they needed to buy food. He added up the money he had, which only came to £49.50. 'I don't know how we're going to make ends meet,' he said.

What does 'make ends meet' mean?

Cont'd

Chris lay on the sofa, eating crisps and watching TV. He had seen the afternoon film, some cartoons, *News Night*, *Neighbours*, *Blue Peter*, a cookery programme, and now he was watching *EastEnders*. His mother told him that he was a couch potato.

What does 'couch potato' mean?

Grandma grew all sorts of flowers and vegetables in her garden. Her runner beans were always better than anyone else's, and her tomatoes were the tastiest. Her garden was always colourful with every possible variety of flower. People said she must have green fingers.

What does having 'green fingers' mean?

'Your room is like a pigsty!' Jan told Caroline. Caroline looked at her sister's room, which could hardly be seen under a pile of clothes, boxes of make-up, magazines and quite a few biscuit wrappers. 'That's the pot calling the kettle black,' she said.

What does it mean if someone says 'the pot is calling the kettle black'?

Freddie ran at Jane, tried to hit her, missed and flung himself on the floor, screaming. 'For goodness sake!' said Jonathan, 'keep your hair on'.

What does 'keep your hair on' mean?

Cont'd

Understanding jokes

What dog has no tail?

A hot dog

What do you get if you cross a kangaroo with a sheep?

A woolly jumper

Why did the man take a pencil to bed?

Because he wanted to draw the curtains

What is grey and has four legs and a trunk?

A mouse going on holiday

Card 1 (top right)

Name: _____ Date: _____

TARGET

Find a simile and metaphor in your book.

Simile:

Metaphor:

Card 2 (bottom right)

Name: _____ Date: _____

TARGET

Write down an idiom your friend used today.

Idiom:

Meaning:

Card 3 (top left)

Name: _____ Date: _____

TARGET

Write down an idiom you heard today.

Idiom:

Meaning:

Card 4 (bottom left)

Name: _____ Date: _____

TARGET

Find words in your book which indicate mood.

Lesson:

Words:

Fact and Opinion

As language develops, children need to be able to distinguish between fact and opinion, non-fiction and fiction, reality and fantasy. While this is usually a feature of normal maturation, for children with language processing difficulties, the boundaries are often less clear.

Weak language skills lead to an over-dependency on information learned from other people. Without the ability to assess the validity of this information, it becomes fact in the child's mind and is maintained dogmatically. As his language skills improve, the child is able to consider other points of view and begins to make judgements.

Much of the curriculum in secondary education relies on the ability to discriminate between fact and opinion. The child cannot be expected to develop and articulate his own opinions, until he can recognise and appreciate the diversity of other people's. Unless he is able to evaluate a range of views, he remains a vulnerable member of his group. A lack of understanding often leads to conflict, both at home and at school.

Do:

- **Explain the difference between fact and opinion.**
  Fact can be proved, while opinions may vary. The child needs to understand that opinions can be different but still valid.

- **Teach the child to recognise the limitations of his knowledge.**
  The child may think that he is an expert on the subject and be unwilling to accept that somebody else, by virtue of age and experience, may know more.

- **Encourage the understanding and appreciation of other people's opinions.**
  The child is more likely to understand differing views, if he is able to appreciate the reasoning process behind them.

- **Examine different ways in which opinions are presented.**
  It is important for the child to recognise how his perceptions are manipulated by, for example, advertisements, magazine and newspaper articles, and television programmes.

Case study 1

Dan, aged 13, was adamant that he could make a fortune by betting on the results of football matches. He based his opinion on the results of private bets with his father, since he was below the age to have been admitted to a betting shop, and refused to acknowledge that there might be a more complicated system involved.

Case study 2

Tony, aged 14, refused to acknowledge that there could be an alternative and valid opinion about whether the war in Iraq was justified. He thought that people who did not support the war were, by implication, condoning the regime.

Resources

1 Joanne Carlisle, *Reasoning and Reading*. Educators Publishing Service Inc. ISBN Level 1 – 0-8388-1813-7; Level 2 – 0-8388-1814-5
2 Lazzari & Myers Peters, *Help* (Handbooks of Exercises for Language Processing). Lingui Systems.
3 *Did you hear that?* Living & Learning (Cambridge) Ltd, distributed by LDA. ISBN 0-905-114698

Opinions

One fact can give rise to many opinions.

Do you agree with the following opinions? What are your opinions?

Fact

Many people keep dogs as pets.

Opinions

- People like pets.
- People like dogs.
- Dogs make good pets.
- Dogs make the best pets.
- Dogs make better pets than cats.
- If you want a pet, it should be a dog.
- There are more dogs kept as pets than any other animal.
- Dogs are easy to care for.
- All dogs are good pets.

Fact

Many young people use recreational drugs.

Opinions

- Young people like taking drugs.
- Older people do not take drugs.
- Young people like to have fun.
- Young people need drugs in order to have fun.
- Drug use is a common activity for young people.
- Young people think drugs are harmless.
- Young people should not risk taking drugs.
- Taking drugs is usually harmless.
- Taking drugs is usually dangerous.

Cont'd

Fact

Football is a popular sport.

Opinions

- Football matches are very exciting.

- Football can be played anywhere.

- Only fit people can play football.

- Many people dislike professional football.

- Football is the best sport on television.

- There is too much football shown on television.

- Footballers earn too much money.

- Football can be played all the year round.

- Football matches are very boring.

- Girls can't play football.

- Football hooligans are dangerous.

- English fans should not be able to go abroad.

- Footballers break more bones than anyone else.

- Anybody can be a professional footballer.

Fact or Opinion?

- Most teenage boys have broken at least one bone in their lives.
- The cornea is part of the eye.
- All dogs like to fight.
- There are 12 months in a year.
- 50 per cent of children in this country cannot read.
- Everyone should have a passport.
- No one who lives in London has a garden.
- The Queen is the richest person in the world.
- Wasps are useless and unnecessary.
- Trains travel on railway lines.
- Atoms can be split.
- Most people learn to drive when they are 17.
- Most English beaches are polluted.
- It's always hot in the summer.
- 9 out of 10 people die of old age.
- Water expands when frozen.
- 1 in 5 people go on holiday.
- Foxes are omnivores.
- All dogs should be allowed to have a litter of puppies.
- Everyone should stay at school until they are 18.
- Everyone can ride a bike.
- James Bond is not a real person.
- Few children will be able to get jobs when they leave school.
- Wheat is used to make bread.
- Everyone likes sweets.
- Half the population of England is boys.
- Grapes are fruit.
- Everyone is vaccinated against whooping cough.
- All boys like to play with cars.
- All the animals in zoos are unhappy.
- People ride camels.
- Antarctica is the coldest continent on earth.
- Some people don't like oysters.
- All children have to go to bed early.
- London is the capital of England.

Cont'd

- How many facts can you find?
- How many opinions can you find?
- How many opinions are likely to be true?
- Could the company prove that the cereal is:
  'packed full of vitamin and fibre'
  'Children love the taste'
  'Mums and Dads love their goodness'?
- Why might children want to buy this cereal?
- In what ways could they be disappointed?

Card 1 (top-left)

Name: _____ Date: _____

TARGET

Find 3 facts from this lesson.

Facts:

1

2

3

Card 2 (top-right)

Name: _____ Date: _____

TARGET

Is your argument based on fact?

Fact:

Teacher's comment:

Card 3 (bottom-left)

Name: _____ Date: _____

TARGET

Is my point fact or opinion?

Fact ☐   Opinion ☐

How do you know?

Because _____

Card 4 (bottom-right)

Name: _____ Date: _____

TARGET

Read a short newspaper article.

What is fact?: _____

What is opinion?: _____

Inference and Prediction

10

Some higher order language difficulties, not noticeable in the earlier years, may only become apparent as the demands of the curriculum increase. Inference is an important feature of secondary education, affecting every subject. The ability to make use of both context and general knowledge is vital.

Inference involves a continual cycle of language processing. The child must listen to what is said and relate this to the context and to his previous knowledge. He must then predict what may come next and, in the light of subsequent information, select one option. He must then discard the other possibilities.

example

The man walked carefully down the path.

The child should ask himself why the man is walking carefully and then make predictions. These might be, for example, that it is icy, that the man is very old, or that the man is carrying something fragile. If the next sentence is 'It was bitterly cold.' then the child should select the first option and discard the others.

The child with language processing difficulties does not have the versatility to undertake such a complex process. In our example, he will probably have understood all the vocabulary in the sentence but not realise the implications of the word 'carefully'. Thus he will not predict what might come next.

Another possibility is that the child may have made suitable predictions but then be unable to discard the inappropriate ones. Thus he may build into his understanding that there is an old man holding something fragile on an icy path. Even if subsequent information indicates that the man is young, he may be unable to change his idea by taking account of the new fact.

Another issue of inferential reasoning is ambiguity. While the child knows more than one meaning of a word, he may be unable to use context to help him select the correct meaning and so will alter his perception of the sentence to suit his interpretation of the word.

example

Hearing a splash, John ran to the bank.

The child may associate the word **bank** with money, and disregard the implications of the word **splash**.

Do:

- **Teach inference as a specific activity.**
  It cannot be assumed that inference will develop naturally. The child with language processing difficulties may reach a limit in his development, which only careful and specific teaching will extend. He needs to learn to ask himself the following questions:

  What do I know?
  What can I predict?
  Am I still right?

● **Use a very small amount of information initially.**
In order to allow the child to concentrate on inference, overloading the child's auditory processing abilities should be avoided. A single sentence can give sufficient material with which to start.

● **Help the child to identify facts from the sentence.**
Children do not always realise how much information they can gain from one sentence. From the example, 'The man walked carefully down the path', the child should be helped to recognise that he knows that:

it is a man not a woman
he is walking not running
he is going down a path not a road
the action takes place outside
there is a need for care.

● **Teach the child the difference between informed prediction and guessing.**
He must learn that while many of his guesses may be possible, unless they are related to some part of the information given, they remain mere guesses rather than predictions.

● **Help the child identify ambiguity.**
It is important to discuss the alternative meanings of a word and why only one meaning is appropriate within the context of the sentence.

● **Discuss possible predictions before giving further information.**
It is often necessary to write down the predictions, to ensure that the child is able to recall all the possibilities and then discard the inappropriate ones.

120

- Teach the child that the modification of his ideas is a constant and necessary process.
  This must initially be a conscious process, so that it may eventually become automatic.

- Teach the child to check and update information consistently.
  When the amount of information increases in length, it is important that the child checks his understanding continually against the facts.

Case study 1

Jonathan, aged 12, was given the following information: 'Steven is hungry, sitting outside his tent. He has a piece of paper and something made of wood. What is he about to do?' Jonathan said, 'Wrap up a parcel.' His guess was supported by only a small part of the information.

Case study 2

The class was told that Mr Hewitt had gone to fetch his glasses and would be back in a few minutes. Sue, aged 13, asked, 'Are we all going to get a drink?'

Resources

1 Arthur J Evans, *Looking and Thinking* 1, 2, 3 and 4. Learning Materials Ltd.

2 Arthur J Evans, *Reading and Thinking* 1, 2, 3 and 4. Learning Materials Ltd.

3 *New Reading and Thinking* 1–5. Learning Materials Ltd. ISBNs: 1 – 1-84198-126-5; 2 – 1-84198-127-5; 3 – 1-84198-128-5; 4 – 1-84198-129-X; 5 – 1-84198-130-3

4 *Did you hear that?* Living & Learning (Cambridge) Ltd, distributed by LDA.

5 Luanne Martin, *Think It – Say It*. Communication Skill Builders. ISBN 0-88450-570-7

6 Sharon G.Webber, *Let's Predict Fun Deck*. Super Duper Publications (Taskmaster).

1. Amy lost her purse on the bus. *What will she do?*

2. Tom sprained his ankle playing football. *What will he do?*

3. I looked in the cupboard, but found I had no flour and no yeast. *What will I do next?*

4. Jack could not see the whiteboard. *What should he do?*

5. Lesley wanted some sweets but did not have any money. *What could she do?*

6. Hayley opened the packet of cereal and a mouse jumped out. *What would she do?*

7. Pat's shoes pinched his toes and hurt his heels. *What might he do?*

8. The bull ran into the street pursued by the farmer. *What will the farmer do?*

9. Alan could not ride his motor bike because he did not have a licence. *What must he do?*

10. The dog scratched behind his ear, he scratched his leg and he scratched his stomach. He rolled in the dust, but it was no use. *What might his owner do?*

11. The village shop was failing. Too many people went to the supermarket in town where prices were cheaper. The owner of the shop could no longer afford an assistant. *What do you think will happen to the shop?*

12. Mrs Jones needed to speak to her doctor, but the phone was out of order? *What could she do?*

Cont'd

13 Sue opened her presents one at a time, making it last as long as possible. She knew that as soon as she had finished, her mum would want her to write letters to her aunts and uncles. *What will she have to do when she has opened her presents?*

14 Ben trudged wearily down the road hoping a bus would pass. He heard the sound of an engine behind him, and turned to see a car coming along the road. *What might he do next?*

15 The tramp sorted through the rubbish bin looking for something to eat. He did not find anything except a £1 coin. *What do you think he did next?*

16 Smoke poured out of the building as they raced for the door. At last they were safely outside. *What did they do next?*

17 John struggled with his maths homework. Mum was no help and Dad was away. He would be in big trouble next day if he had not finished it. *What could he do?*

18 It rained and rained. The tent was wet inside and outside and it seemed as if a river was running through it. *What might the people in the tent do next?*

19 Ned tripped over the pot of green paint as he walked through the house, and it spilt all over the pale pink carpet. *What should he do next?*

20 Nick wondered what time the next train to London was, and whether he would have time to stop off at the shop on the way to the station. *What will he do next?*

What do I Know?

What do I know? What can I infer/guess?

Children, who are poor at making inferences often fail to recognise what they definitely know, what is an informed guess (inference) and what is a wild guess. Working on one sentence at a time gives the child an achievable target on which to practise.

Read one sentence at a time, working out with the child what he knows and what is an informed guess. Read the next sentence and decide which informed guesses must be discarded and which can be confirmed.

Examples

● **He climbed slowly upwards.**

What do we know?
 a The person is male.
 b He was climbing slowly.

What can we infer/guess?
 a He was probably outside.
 b What he was climbing was steep, or the weather was hot or he was old.

● **He breathed in the thin mountain air.**

What do we know?
 a He is on a mountain. (Confirm: he was outside)
 b He breathed thin air.

What can we infer/guess?
 a He is fairly high up the mountain because the air is thin.
 b He is climbing slowly because of the thin air. (Discard: it was hot or he was old. Keep: he was climbing something steep but that is not why he climbed slowly.)

Cont'd

● **He looked up, saw the nearby summit of the mountain, and smiled.**

What do we know?
  a He was near the top of the mountain. (Confirm: he is high up)
  b He smiled.

What can we infer/guess?
  a He smiled because he was pleased that he had nearly reached his goal.

Suggested sentences

1 'I'll just get my bag,' she said, 'you get in the car.'
'Is it far to the zoo?' asked Cleo, as Mum started the car and put her handbag on the seat.

2 She flew through the trees searching for food. The cold weather had killed many of the insects. Unless she could find food soon, her young would die.

3 Water gushed everywhere. 'Turn off the main,' Dad shouted. 'Call the plumber!' Mum shouted. David huddled further into his bed and pretended to be asleep.

Resources

Reading and Thinking (Books 1 to 5) by Arthur J Evans published by Learning Materials Ltd. are an excellent source of material for these exercises.

Bus Queue

Inference

(See picture on next page.)

1 Who feels the cold?

2 Who has been shopping?

3 Who probably does not work, and why?

4 How many people need to see an optician regularly?

5 Who probably has an old age pension?

6 Who visits the hairdresser regularly?

7 Who probably goes to work each day?

8 Who will have a bus pass?

9 Who will pay half fare?

10 Who will travel free?

11 Who has been waiting the longest?

12 Who has been waiting the shortest?

13 Who is a mother?

14 Who might be at school?

15 Who might be at college?

16 Who works in an office?

17 Who thought it might rain?

18 Who is smartly dressed?

19 Who is bored?

20 How many people are having a conversation?

21 Who is fashionably dressed?

22 Who should be particularly careful not to get sunburned?

23 Who is younger than the boy sitting on the pavement?

24 Whose shoes would not be worn in winter?

25 Whose trousers might have been mended?

26 Who might be going to stay with friends?

27 Who might be taking the bus to the station?

28 Who might be going home?

29 Who might be going to the cinema?

30 Whose clothes would not be appropriate for working in an office?

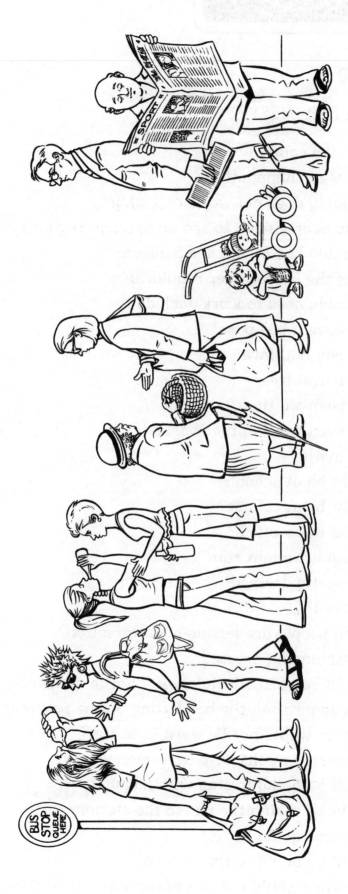

Yes or No?

Is there enough information in the following sentences to enable you to answer the question? You can only answer 'Yes', 'No' or 'I need more information'.

1. The teacher wondered whether the whole class would be able to do the experiment.
   Did the class do the experiment?

2. None of the team scored a goal on Saturday.
   Did the team win the match?

3. Paul could not wait to see if he had been given a bike for his birthday.
   Was Paul given a bike for his birthday?

4. Sue promised she would find the book when she went home.
   Did Sue find the book?

5. The man, who bought his ticket the day before from Edinburgh, arrived safely in Glasgow.
   Did the man have a ticket?

6. Tom could not believe that he had not won the race.
   Did Tom win the race?

7. We wanted to know if we would be able to go to the beach, if the rain stopped.
   Could we go to the beach?

8. The boys should not have gone out last night.
   Did the boys go out last night?

9. Anna and John thought the rock concert was wonderful but Sam disagreed.
   Did Sam enjoy the concert?

10. I could visit you on Wednesday, although you would prefer me to come on Tuesday.
    Did I visit on Tuesday?

Descriptions

What do we know about each person from the following descriptions?

1. Mrs Jones, her grey hair in a bun, searched in her purse for enough money to put in the gas meter.

2. John trudged wearily home, trailing his bag, worrying about the next day.

3. He was getting very anxious as the food was running out and his radio batteries were flat.

4. Sara applied her make-up thoroughly, careful not to over do it, as she thought about the qualities needed for the job.

5. Jogging down the road, Kate worried that she looked fat and unattractive in her tracksuit.

6. Ben climbed onto the sofa, holding a biscuit carefully in his left hand.

7. Pulling on his gloves, and wishing he had thought to bring a scarf, Tom climbed on to the tractor and turned the key.

8. Amy pulled at the door with all her strength. She could hardly reach the handle, even standing on tiptoe, but she tried as hard as she could, knowing she would be in trouble if she was late home. There was an old fashioned clock on the wall, which she could not read because it had Roman numerals, but the sky was definitely getting darker. She pushed the tangled hair out of her eyes, and wiped a grimy hand over her face, determined not to cry.

Cont'd

9   The castle stood cold and still. He drifted through the rooms as though moved by a current of air and glided through the closed door into the banqueting hall, silent now and lifeless. With an absent minded sigh, he took off his head and tucked it more comfortably under his arm, as he remembered back to the days when the castle was full of warmth and excitement.

10   They kept up a steady pace, moving quietly through the trees, out of sight of the road. Bess wrinkled her nose and sniffed the morning air, trying to catch some scent that would tell them in which direction to go.

11   Tall, muscular and strong though he was, Ben was at a disadvantage climbing the tree. The leopard climbed faster and more confidently and was gaining on him fast.

12   He remembered his 60th birthday as though it were yesterday. His wife had still been alive then and they had danced all evening. The thought of dancing now was impossible. Even his fingers were stiff, and his legs would barely hold up his weight just walking.

● How many people were involved in the accident?

● What happened to the dog?

● To whom does the dog belong?

● Do you think the dog is hurt?

● Where will the owner take the dog if it is hurt?

● Will the owner have to pay to have the dog made better?

● Why do you think the accident happened?

TARGET

Name: _____ Date: _____

Is your interpretation the only one?

Yes ☐   No ☐

If no, give one other interpretation.

TARGET

Name: _____ Date: _____

Do you need to change your opinion?

Yes ☐   No ☐

TARGET

Name: _____ Date: _____

Are you guessing?

Yes ☐   No ☐

If yes, why did you make that guess?

TARGET

Name: _____ Date: _____

What do I know?
What can I predict?
Am I still right?

Non-verbal Language

A large part of effective communication is non-verbal. Apart from the obvious use of gesture and facial expression, other features, such as body language and voice production, help to clarify meaning. It is much easier to listen to a speaker with good non-verbal language skills, since the information is conveyed through both the visual and auditory pathways. The inability to read non-verbal language has significant social implications.

Gesture is a deliberate feature of communication, used to back up the intended meaning. It is often a great help for children with verbal processing difficulties because it reinforces the information through a different pathway.

Facial expression gives additional information about the mood or feelings of the speaker, and is a natural feature of communication. However, some people's faces are less expressive than others, which causes problems for the child who relies on this adjunct to communication.

Intonation, **stress and volume** are the three significant areas of voice production which convey meaning. Intonation patterns indicate the type of information which is being given, such as a statement or a question, a comment or a reprimand, a demand or a plea. Stress is used to indicate the significant words in a sentence, and is therefore a useful feature, when talking to children with processing difficulties. Appropriate volume is another way of adding variety and shades of meaning to speech. There are likely to be a number of children in the class, who have a mild residual hearing loss, due to recurrent glue ear problems when younger, and for these, sufficient volume of speech is important.

Children, who are able to read non-verbal language, can recognise the mood of teachers, parents and peers, predict possible consequences and modify their behaviour accordingly. Those who cannot do this, often feel that punishment is unfair, as they have been unable to recognise 'the last straw'.

Do:

- **Make use of gesture to help children understand more easily.**
  This develops the ability to focus on the teacher and understand what is being said.

- **Make sure your gesture is readily understood.**
  As well as making use of pointing etc., use more specific gesture to clarify meaning, e.g. when asking for particular dimensions, indicate the required size with your hands.

- **Make active use of facial expression.**
  A variety of facial expressions help the child focus on the speaker and gain added information.

- **Vary your intonation, stress and volume appropriately.**
  Children are more likely to maintain their interest in what you are saying if your presentation is more animated.

- **Use stress to emphasise the important vocabulary in a sentence.**
  The child with weaker language processing skills finds it difficult to take in longer pieces of information, so will need help to focus on the important parts.

- **Vary your intonation and volume to suit different situations.**
  Many children respond to a quieter voice as well as a louder one. It is the variation that is important.

- **Be consistent in your use of non-verbal language.**
  The child who has difficulty following non-verbal language, needs to learn to associate your behaviour with a particular mood. For example, if you raise your voice this may be an indication that you are becoming irritated. However, if you use a raised voice too often, its significance is diluted.

- **Be aware that some children are very sensitive to noise.**
  Some children, such as those diagnosed with Asperger Syndrome, become extremely distressed in a noisy environment. They particularly dislike being shouted at by teachers or peers.

- **Warn the child overtly when his behaviour is becoming unacceptable.**
  Since he has difficulty understanding non-verbal language, the signal needs to be concrete. This could be a traffic light system or a private signal between the teacher and the pupil, such as a tap on the shoulder or desk.

- **Help the child to recognise from his friends' non-verbal language, when his behaviour is becoming irritating.**
  He may be puzzled and upset by what he sees as his friends' inexplicable and unreasonable reaction. This is often the cause of turmoil.

- Use a concrete system to show the child how often he is producing unacceptable behaviour.
  The child often does not realise how many times he has been told to stop a behaviour and therefore needs help to monitor his own behaviour. This is most effectively achieved by marking down on a card each time the behaviour is repeated.

Case study 1

David, aged 12, felt aggrieved when reprimanded for shouting out an answer in class. He had not recognised that the teacher was becoming increasingly irritated by this behaviour in other pupils and that his shout was 'the last straw'.

Case study 2

Freddie, aged 16, interrupted a class in which an army officer was making a presentation. The teacher asked him quietly not to do it again. Freddie, not recognising the seriousness of the situation, came in again and was reproved more actively by the teacher. However, he came in a third time to fetch a book and was distraught and mortified by the army officer's strong reaction. Freddie had completely failed to read the non-verbal signals given by his teacher.

Resources

1   Photo Emotion cards, LDA
2   Ian Franklin, *Let's Mime* (cards). Winslow.

Using Intonation

Try saying these sentences using different intonation, and ask the child how he thinks you feel from the tone of your voice. It may be necessary to over emphasise at first in order to help him to appreciate the differences.

What are you doing?
Change the intonation by stressing a different word each time so that the question can be indignant, surprised, accusing or puzzled.

Coming downstairs, she fell over the cat and dropped the tray.
Say this as if telling a hilarious story, or as a serious accident.

It's not mine.
Suggest indifference or indignation.

You're late.
This could be accusing, interested or worried.

I haven't heard from him since he went to Birmingham.
Stress 'I' to sound anxious or angry. Even stress will suggest indifference.

Don't do that.
Say this as an exclamation, implying a risk if the listener disobeys. Stress on 'don't' may sound quelling or displeased. Even stress could indicate a quiet aside to remind the person spoken to, without alerting the whole class.

Cont'd

I think you need to go over that exercise again.

Stress 'I' as if giving a personal opinion, use even intonation to convey a friendly suggestion, and more emphasis to indicate displeasure.

Sit down quietly.

Try this as an angry command or a routine reminder.

I told you to finish the exercise before going out to break.

Use anger, patient re-iteration, or emphasize 'I' to show that it was your instruction, not anyone else's.

What did you do?

This can be angry and confrontational, or as an interested query.

The Headmaster says he saw you in the Drama room.

This could be said accusingly, or in a neutral tone conveying information, or pleased, as if the child had, perhaps, been seen in a play.

I'm not prepared to do that.

This could convey that you are not yet ready, or do not have the right equipment, or that you will not even consider this request.

Non-verbal Language

Games and exercises to help the understanding of non-verbal language.

Wink murder

Eye pointing 1

The teacher faces the group of children and gives them each a number. She then taps or claps a number and gives the child who has that number a non-verbal (gesture or pointing) command.

Eye pointing 2

Each child takes it in turn to ask a question, using eye contact to indicate who should answer.

Miming emotion

Each child acts out a way of doing an action, e.g. walking wearily, slowly, briskly, etc., for the rest of the group to guess.

Miming actions

Miming actions such as chopping wood, cleaning teeth, umpiring a football match, serving in a shop, painting a gate, etc.

Interpreting facial expression

Cut out photos from newspapers and magazines which show a range of emotions.

1 Discuss with the child what emotions are shown in the pictures.
2 Ask the child to group the pictures according to mood, or to grade them from positive to negative emotions.
3 The child is given a sentence. The teacher mimes a facial expression. The child must then decide how the teacher would say the sentence, and then attempt to say it in that manner.

Interpreting action without sound

Watch a short video without the sound, then discuss with the child what he thought was happening. Re-play the video with sound and discuss any misunderstandings.

Mood Lines

Mood lines help the child to express his emotions in a non-verbal way and to recognise how his behaviour affects others.

The child and the teacher each have a mood line. One half of each line is in a negative colour (perhaps black or red) to indicate negative or unhappy feelings and the other is in a favourite colour to indicate positive or happy feelings. Neutral feelings are where the two colours meet.

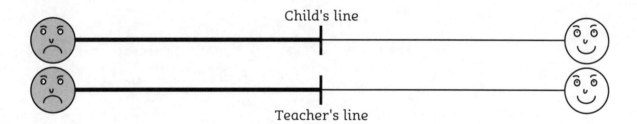

Child's line

Teacher's line

Each lesson the child and teacher draw a new mood line, discuss how they feel, and mark this on the line.

The teacher should generally start from the centre, where the two colours meet, suggesting that her mood is neutral and balanced. The child is quite likely to want to start at either extreme, and needs to be led through the process of recognising that his present mood is not as bad, for instance, as if his dog had just been run over, or as good as if he had just been given a new quad bike.

Cont'd

As the lesson progresses the teacher shows the child how his work or behaviour is affecting the way she feels, and marks it on her line. For example, the teacher may feel pleased because the child has worked hard, and therefore she feels 'further along' the positive line. This in turn may affect how the child feels about himself, making him more positive. On the other hand, inattention by the child may irritate the teacher, who demonstrates on her line that she is now less happy than at the start of the lesson. The child, able to see the effect of his behaviour, may now try harder, which in turn affects the teacher's mood.

By the end of the lesson, both lines should have arrows running down, then back up etc. giving a visual picture of how the emotions have changed.

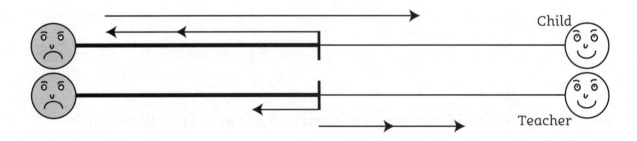

As the child becomes accustomed to using the mood line, the activity can be extended to discuss emotional situations that occur elsewhere.

How Do They Feel?

Think of two words to describe:

● How the woman feels.

● How the man driving the car feels.

● How the man watching the accident feels.

● How the dog feels.

● How you would feel if it was your dog.

TARGET

Name: _____   Date: _____

Am I reading the signs?

Look at: facial expression
          body language

Listen to: intonation

TARGET

Name: _____   Date: _____

Stop before I get into trouble.

TARGET

Name: _____   Date: _____

Am I over-reacting?

☐☐☐☐☐☐☐☐☐☐☐
☐☐☐☐☐☐☐☐☐☐☐

TARGET

Name: _____   Date: _____

How does your teacher feel?

Happy ———————————————— Angry

   Listening and Understanding in Secondary Schools   11 Non-verbal Language

The Language of Maths

There are children who fail in maths not because they are unable to grasp the mathematical concept but because they do not comprehend the verbal labels and the underlying linguistic concepts. This might affect the understanding of the names given to numbers, the variety of words associated with a single symbol or process, or the complexity of the subject-specific vocabulary. Mental arithmetic is particularly taxing.

Difficulty in labelling numbers can be an unrecognised problem. While there are instances of children being unable to match the name to the symbol, the more common problem in older children is a confusion between similar words, such as 'eighteen' and 'eighty'. Children who process language poorly do not always hear the small difference in pronunciation, despite knowing the difference in value when reading the symbol.

It is often assumed that the basic maths vocabulary will have been established in primary school. However, some children fail to achieve this because of weak language processing skills and are then further confused by the necessity of learning several words for one symbol, such as: *take away, minus, less, reduce, decrease*. This applies similarly to the language of shapes, both 2-dimensional and 3-dimensional, probability, measurement, statistics, graphs, geometry, algebra and trigonometry.

Difficulties in understanding language concepts such as comparatives and superlatives, sequential, spatial and temporal vocabulary may have a significant effect on mathematical processing.

Mental arithmetic puts a heavy load on comprehension because of a number of reasons. The child with slow processing is unable to take in all the information. The child with poor working memory is unable to hold the information in the short term, while undertaking the calculation. In both cases, the unfamiliar vocabulary and the density of information are additional problems to be overcome.

Do:

- **Check that a difficulty in maths is not based on a labelling confusion.**
  Unless the basic vocabulary is fully established, the child will be unable to progress through the subsequent stages.

- **Base verbal problems on the child's experience.**
  This will enable the child to picture the problem and reduce the reliance on language processing.

- **Give word banks of the variety of vocabulary associated with a single concept or symbol.**
  This removes the additional problem of having to recall the meanings of the words, so that the child can concentrate on the mathematical process. It also helps to reinforce the vocabulary.

- **Check that the child has clearly heard and understood the difference between number values.**
  This is particularly significant for 14 and 40, 16 and 60, 18 and 80, etc.

- **Introduce new vocabulary carefully.**
  New words should be written on the board with examples, so that the child has both the auditory, visual and written reinforcement.

- Check that the child understands the concept of comparatives and superlatives.

  The concept of more/most and less/least is often a confusing one.

- Grade mental arithmetic problems carefully.

  Initially, it may be necessary to give written clues. Problems should be given in short manageable chunks, enabling the child to process more effectively.

Case study 1

Joe, aged 13, could cope with maths as long as the question was written down, but made errors in mental arithmetic because he was slow to associate numbers with their labels, particularly *-ty* and *-teen*.

Case study 2

Chris, aged 16, in the GCSE exam, was unable to relate the process of finding a percentage (which he could do) to the question because of the complexity of the language.

Resources

1 Sheila Gallagher, *Talking Maths* photographs. LDA.
2 *The Maths Language Pack*, Cutting Edge Publications, Pill Farmhouse, Lostwithiel, Cornwall PL22 0JR.

Shapes

Find the names of the shapes in the wordsearch.

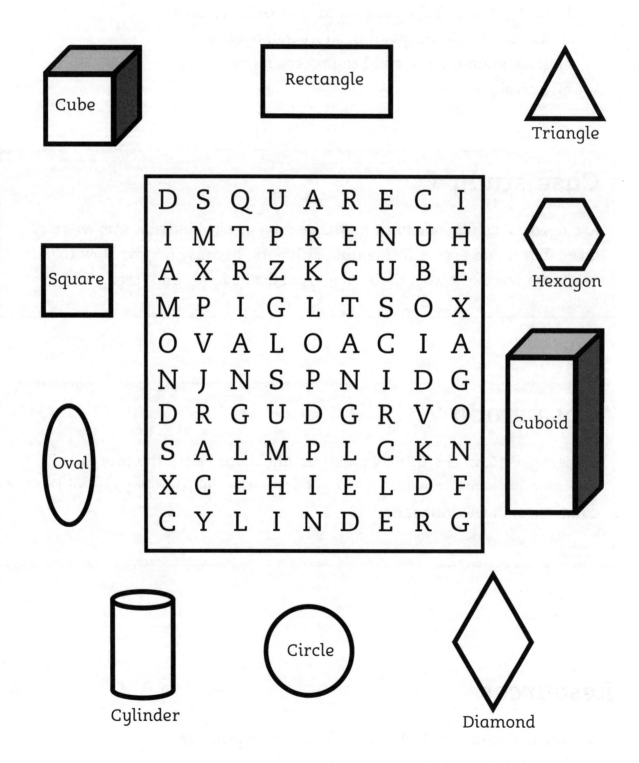

Cube

Rectangle

Triangle

Square

Hexagon

D	S	Q	U	A	R	E	C	I
I	M	T	P	R	E	N	U	H
A	X	R	Z	K	C	U	B	E
M	P	I	G	L	T	S	O	X
O	V	A	L	O	A	C	I	A
N	J	N	S	P	N	I	D	G
D	R	G	U	D	G	R	V	O
S	A	L	M	P	L	C	K	N
X	C	E	H	I	E	L	D	F
C	Y	L	I	N	D	E	R	G

Cuboid

Oval

Cylinder

Circle

Diamond

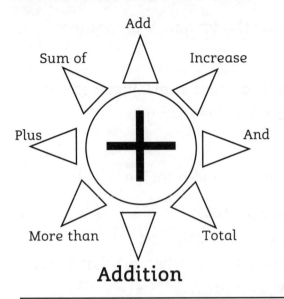

Addition

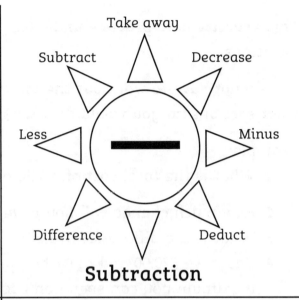

Subtraction

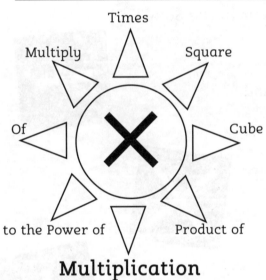

Multiplication

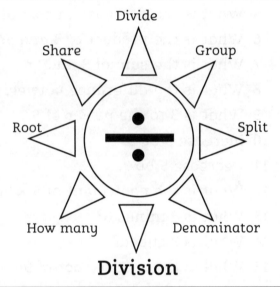

Division

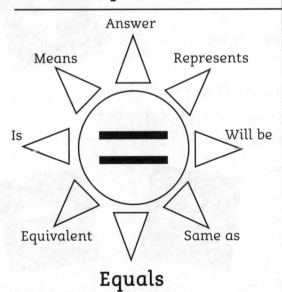

Equals

Additional

Subtraction

Division

Multiplication

Equals

What Sort of Sum?

This exercise is to practise understanding the language of maths in questions.

You do **not** have to work out the answers to these sums, just work out what sort of sum you would do. Question 1 is done for you.

Example:

1 What is the total cost of a kilo of apples and a melon? **(+)**

2 How much change will you have from £3.00?

3 What is the difference in height between Susie and Jo?

4 You have £20.00 and must buy presents for 3 friends. What is the maximum you can spend on each present?

5 What is the decrease in cost of a coat in the Sale?

6 What is the product of 3 and 5?

7 What is the sum of 3 and 5?

8 What is the difference between 3 and 5?

9 What is 3 to the power of 5?

10 Increase 3 by 5.

11 Decrease 5 by 3.

12 What is the equivalent of 5×3?

13 What is 5 minus 3?

14 What is 3 cubed?

15 What is the square root of 9?

16 Multiply the sum of 4 and 6 by 5.

17 What is the sum of 4 and 6, squared?

18 Deduct 4 from 6 squared.

19 Which is more: 5 deducted from 10 or 10 increased by 5?

20 What is the mathematical term that is the opposite to plus?

21 What is the mathematical term that is the opposite to divide?

22 Find the perimeter of a pentagon.

23 Find the area of a rectangle.

24 Find the circumference of a circle.

Check your answer is possible.

Should the answer be bigger than the number I started with?

Should the answer be smaller than the number I started with?

Did you understand the question?

ASK.

What sort of sum is this?

+ _____

− _____

× _____

÷ _____

Underline all the words which mean:

Add

Take away

Multiply

Divide

Bibliography

Adams, C. 'Clinical diagnostic and intervention studies of children with semantic–pragmatic disorder'. *International Journal of Language and Communication Disorders*, Vol. 6 No. 3 July–Sept 2001.

Bishop, D.V.M. *Uncommon Understanding; Development and Disorders of Language Comprehension in Children.* Psychology Press. ISBN 0-86377-501-2

Crystal, D. *The Cambridge Encyclopaedia of Language.* Cambridge University Press. ISBN 0-521-42443-7

Letts, C. and Leinonen, E. 'Comprehension of inferential meaning in language-impaired children and language normal children'. *International Journal of Language and Communication Disorders*, Vol. 6 No. 3 July–Sept 2001.

Lindamood, P. and Lindamood, P. *The Lindamood Phoneme Sequencing Program for reading, spelling and speech. (LiPS)* (3rd edition). Pro-ed Taskmaster Ltd. ISBN 0-89079-753-6

McTear, M.F. and Conti-Ramsden G. *Pragmatic Disability in Children.* Whurr Publishers Ltd. ISBN 187-0332-768

Stackhouse, J. and Wells, B. (Eds), *Children's Speech and Literacy Difficulties 2: Identification and Intervention.* Whurr Publications. ISBN 186-156-1318

Van der Lely, H.K.J. 'Specific language impairment in children: research findings and their therapeutic implications'. *European Journal of Disorders of Communication.* Vol. 28 No. 3, 1993.

Wiig, E.H. and Semel, E. *Language Assessment and Intervention for the Learning Disabled* (2nd edition). Charles E. Merrill Publishing Co. ISBN 0-675-20124-1

Index